KT-102-876

PICTORIAL
GARDENING

PICTORIAL GARDENING

With over 1,300 how-to-do-it photographs

COLLINGRIDGE BOOKS

LONDON · NEW YORK · SYDNEY · TORONTO

© C. Arthur Pearson Ltd 1938
© Thirteenth Revised Edition
The Hamlyn Publishing Group Ltd 1969

First published 1938
Thirteenth Revised Edition 1969
Third Impression 1972

Published for Collingridge Books by
THE HAMLYN PUBLISHING GROUP LTD
LONDON · NEW YORK · SYDNEY · TORONTO
Hamlyn House, Feltham, Middlesex, England

ISBN 0 600 42209 7

MADE AND PRINTED BY OFFSET IN GREAT BRITAIN BY
WILLIAM CLOWES & SONS, LIMITED
LONDON, BECCLES AND COLCHESTER

CONTENTS

ACKNOWLEDGMENTS

Grateful acknowledgment is made to Shell International Petroleum Company Ltd., Murphy Chemical Company Ltd., Long Ashton Research Station and *Amateur Gardening* for permission to reproduce photographs which appear in this book.

INTRODUCTION

Many of the garden jobs that usually seem intricate and difficult to carry out when described in an article or book are in fact surprisingly simple. The ideal way for an amateur to learn both the basic techniques and the finer points of flower, fruit and vegetable growing is for him to be *shown* by an expert.

Few ordinary gardeners, unfortunately, have the chance to learn in this way. The gardening films and film strips often used by Horticultural Societies are very useful, and so too are the radio and television programmes that can be seen and heard at home. But all suffer from one basic disadvantage; they cannot by their very nature be on hand when they are actually most needed—when the particular task they describe is being done.

How, then, is the amateur, full of enthusiasm but lacking knowledge of the technical side of gardening, to familiarise himself with the many operations needed to develop to the full the beauty and productivity possible with even the smallest and most unpromising site?

Good clear photographs specially taken for the purpose are the answer. Such pictures combine many of the advantages of personal instruction with the technical value of films and television. One good picture can often give at a glance information that could not be so effectively acquired from pages of print.

Pictorial Gardening is entirely composed of demonstration photographs, covering each and every branch of garden maintenance and management. Study the pictures at leisure, or take the book into the garden with you when any special work is on hand. Carefully followed, *Pictorial Gardening* will help you to get close to your own idea of a perfect garden. No gardener, of course, can ever be entirely content with his achievements; next year always offers the glittering prospect of improving on perfection!

GARDEN MAINTENANCE

PREPARING THE SITE FOR A NEW GARDEN

Left—When a new garden is being planned from scratch, differing levels often have to be taken into account. *Below*—Tree stumps on a new site are best dug out. To hasten rotting bore holes 6–8 in. deep and the same distance apart, and fill with hydrochloric acid. The tops of the holes should be sealed off with clay. Renew the acid application 2–3 times.

Above—Clearing off long grass and tall weeds is often the first job, and such material can usually be added to a compost heap. Note the 6-ft-by-6-ft panels forming the boundary screen. Once the initial clearance has been done, this allows the plot to be dug, ploughed or rotavated. *Right*—Dealing with an existing or neglected garden often means starting again, and the first job is to find out what you have to deal with—stones, brickbats or other rubbish needs to be sorted out. Such material is useful for path making.

CLEARING AND LEVELLING

Left—Where a large area has to be dealt with, a flame gun can be used to burn off old grass, weeds, brambles and other similar rubbish. A small area can be dealt with by cutting with a grass hook, burning any unwanted material and composting the rest. *Below*—Checking with a spirit level to obtain the initial level, which is especially important where a new lawn is to be made. This aspect is dealt with in later pages.

Above—Obtain the first level by filling in hollows and reducing small raised areas, where possible using any soil excavated from a path site to adjust levels. *Right*—Marking out where a path is to be made. If a considerable amount of wheelbarrow work is anticipated, a concrete or other hard path ensures easier working when moving stones, soil, rubbish or manure.

WALLS AND STEPS

Right—A low retaining wall is especially useful in linking one level of the garden to another when a slope or bank is being dealt with. Cavities can be left for trailing rock plants like *Alyssum saxatile* or *Aubrieta*. *Below*—Building the initial steps, the concrete being kept in place with shuttering boards until set. Steps of about 9 in. are adequate.

Above—The base of each step is filled with concrete. Here the actual step is being faced with crazy paving stone. *Left*—Space can be left between crazy paving stones for low-growing plants like dwarf thyme. If a concrete finish is preferred, do not smooth off the final surface too much, otherwise the steps may be slippery in wet weather.

PATH MAKING—I

Right—When the excavation has been completed, fill in the base with a 3-in. layer of stones, brickbats and the like. Break up any large pieces and leave roughly level. *Below*—Fix boards upright at the sides of the path. These must be kept rigid by pegs driven in as shown.

Above—Ensure that the finished level will be accurate by keeping the side boards adjusted, using a spirit level to maintain accuracy. *Left*—The path can be made up in sections, each length of concrete being 3 ft or so. Lay a strip of roofing felt between each section as shown.

PATH MAKING—2

Right—Checking level of boards at side of path as work progresses. A 3-in. thickness of concrete is adequate. For use in quantity it can be bought "ready mixed", but for small amounts home mixing is best. *Below*—Add small quantities from a bucket, or shovel from a barrow, working in short lengths at a time.

Above—Firm down the wet concrete with a straight edge, adjusting levels to the height of the side boards. Close attention to this final finish is important. *Left*—Continue the work in sections, only removing side boards from the finished work when the laid concrete is dry. The side boards can then be relaid for the next section.

Right—Broken paving stone can usually be purchased for crazy paving. The stones are laid on a layer of sand or ashes, and the spaces between filled with cement, mortar or soil where carpeting plants are to be grown.

Right—Path-making material like Decopath for laying on a hard surface is easily purchased. Here the coloured chippings are being rolled in to give the finished appearance, which is very decorative.

TYPES OF PATHS

Left—A path made from concrete slabs is easiest to make, and slabs can be purchased in varying sizes. A path can often be made from a single width of 2-ft-by-2-ft slabs.

Left—A concrete path can be laid, then marked off in squares whilst the concrete is still damp, to give the appearance of slabs or crazy paving.

PERGOLAS AND RUSTIC SCREENS—I

Left—Posts can be driven into the soil much more easily if they are sharpened with an axe or saw.

Right—After the base of a stake has been sharpened, remove the bark with a spoke-shave. This allows for easier treatment with creosote or other wood preservative.

Left—Wood posts being treated with creosote at the base. This ensures a longer life by prevention of rotting. More than one application should be given, brushing in well each time.

PERGOLAS AND RUSTIC SCREENS—2

Right—Stout nails being driven home after first making holes part way with a brace and bit. This method prevents splitting. *Below*—When cross pieces are nailed to the main supports, cut them to the right angle before erection.

Above—Posts can be kept rigid and upright by setting stones around the base. These should be pushed into place firmly with the end of a stake. *Left*—For very rigid fixing, set the bases of the main stakes in concrete. First tack two or three supporting pieces to the main stake to keep it upright.

SETTING POSTS

Left—One method of making holes for pergola posts or to support wires is to use a post hole borer.

Right—Where posts are to support wires, as for climbing roses or fruit trees, make sure that they are set in line. Here posts are being "lined up" before wires are fitted.

Left—Setting a post by firming the soil at the base with a short stake. This should be done a little at a time, i.e. not all from the final surface. Make the soil firm all round the base of the post.

Right—End posts can be made fully firm by using an end support. Set this at an angle; its base can be set in concrete if necessary.

Right—Push each bolt through and fit with a washer. Put on a nut, taking a couple of turns of the thread only.

TRAINING WIRES

Left—Where wires are to be used for training climbing roses, first bore holes at regular intervals up the post to take the eye-bolts.

Left—Take the end of the straining wire and feed through the eye twice, twist the spare end over and pinch firmly together. By holding the eye of the bolt with pliers and tightening the nut, the wire is made taught.

Right—Upright posts to which interwoven fencing panels are attached can easily become loose through movement caused by the panels moving in the wind. It is advisable to brace each post to avoid this while the cement is setting.

Right—Use a wooden rake to break down the soil and to obtain the tilth (fine surface) needed for sowing. Several such rakings should be given, but only when the soil is dry. Remove any stones whilst raking.

PREPARING A LAWN
FOR SOWING
Left—Lawn seed can be sown in late August or early September, or in spring. Dig the site about a month before sowing to allow for settlement. Tread small and roll large areas when the soil is dry, to break down lumps and to give even firmness.

Left—Use an iron or springbok-type rake to obtain the final tilth. A base dressing of fertiliser can be raked into the soil surface at this stage. A suitable mixture is 2 oz. superphosphate, 1 oz. sulphate of ammonia and 1 oz. sulphate of potash, all to the square yard.

Right—Roll to obtain the final level and then give a further raking with an iron rake. Aim at an even level with no bumps or hollows, and even tilth over all the plot.

SOWING A LAWN BY HAND

Below—To simplify sowing a lawn by hand the plot is best marked off into yard-wide strips with string. These strips can then be measured off to find the number of square yards.

Above—Before sowing the strips, work from one end backwards, raking the ground down to an even level and tilth. Ensure that footmarks are removed.

Below—Having marked out the number of square yards in each strip and determined the rate of sowing (say 2 oz. per sq. yd), place the seed in a bowl. Take a handful and scatter the seed evenly, hand kept close to the ground.

Above—Most of the good seed offered today is treated against its biggest enemy—birds. But it is still a help to germination to cover it in by lightly raking over the ground. Both sowing and raking should be done from a board.

SOWING A LAWN BY MACHINE

Left—For large areas, a Quillot may be used for seed sowing. Seed today is in most cases treated against birds. Shake it well to ensure that it is well mixed with the deterrent.

Right—Load the hopper with the required amount of seed. The rate of distribution is controlled by changeable roller bars. The Quillot is sold with extra bars for this purpose.

Left—Sowing in progress. With the Quillot even distribution is assured, and large areas can be dealt with quickly and evenly. Sowing rate advised is $1\frac{1}{2}$ to 2 oz. per sq. yd.

Right—After sowing, lightly rake the whole area with an iron or metal-toothed springbok rake to give protection from birds. Seed should be only just covered.

PRE-SOWN AND CREEPING GRASS LAWNS

Below — Pre-sown seed in strips of paper material, which later rots, is laid in position on a site prepared as for seed sowing. A useful method where birds are troublesome.

Above—After laying, water the strips evenly to ensure quick germination. It is best to use a rosed watering can for this purpose.

Below—After watering, lightly cover the strips with fine, fairly dry soil distributed through a sieve, using planks set alongside to stand on.

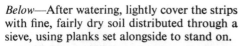

Above—Emerald Velvet, a type of creeping grass, is useful for establishing a lawn. Here newly planted clumps are sending out shoots. Soil preparation before planting is as for grass seed. Plant in autumn, winter or early spring.

TURFING

Right—Soil preparation should be as for sowing seed. The turves are laid so that each interlocks as shown. They should be placed together touching, but here are spaced well apart to show the method of laying. *Below*—Laying the turf. Do not buy cheap turf, which may contain coarse grasses and perennial weeds. It is best to lay turf in autumn so that it has the maximum time to knit together and to establish fresh roots. Water in a dry spell in spring.

Below left—Any spaces between the turves should be filled in with fine soil to encourage the knitting together of individual turves. This will also prevent cracking in dry weather in spring and summer. *Below right*—Consolidation by use of a rammer. A light roller may be used as an alternative. Do not use a very heavy roller or roll when the turf is wet.

TREATING BARE PATCHES

Left—The first method is to cut the bare piece out and replace. This can be done at any time, but best in autumn or winter. In warm summer conditions, keep well watered.

Right—Remove the cut patch by lightly forking up the base, then if necessary fill in the hole with soil to raise the level before the square of turf is relaid.

Left—The second method is to fork up the area and resow, adding fresh soil if necessary. Leave the new soil level slightly below the old to allow for covering in. Sow liberally.

Right—Cover the seed by sieving some soil over it to a depth of $\frac{1}{4}$ in. This will prevent loss by birds. Water the newly sown area in dry conditions so that the new grass is established quickly.

LEVELLING DEPRESSIONS

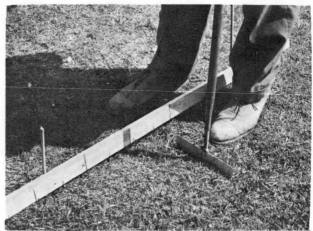

Right—Ascertain depression areas by using a straight edge, then cut the turf into convenient-sized squares in readiness for lifting. *Below*—Lift the turves from the area to be levelled, cutting all turves to equal thickness.

Above—Fill in the hollows with fresh soil and level evenly, firming moderately before the turf is replaced. *Left*—Replace the turf in position and check that the final level is correct. This type of renovation work is best done in autumn; it should be avoided when the soil is dry.

REPAIRING LAWN EDGES

Below—Cut a square from the portion of the edge which is damaged, sink the spade blade to a depth of 2 in. and lift the square.

Above—Move the cut square forward so that the damaged portion extends well beyond the edge of the lawn.

Below—Trim off with an edging tool or a spade so that a fresh unbroken edge is obtained.

Above—Fill in the remaining space with a fresh piece of turf cut to size. If none is available, fill in with fresh soil, make firm and level, and sow grass seed on the patch as soon as possible, watering in dry weather.

LAWN MAINTENANCE

Right—Raking out moss and dead grass with a springbok rake in autumn. Moss is often worse in a shaded area or where the soil tends to lie rather damp. Very close mowing can also lead to growth of moss. *Below*— Spiking with an ordinary fork to improve aeration. This also allows a dressing of soil, peat, or sand and soil to be brushed in to fill the holes. Such a top dressing is of particular benefit on a neglected lawn.

Above—Brushing worm casts with a birch broom in autumn to level out the soil from the casts. If these are left and weather is wet, they leave a muddy mark on the grass. *Left*—Do not allow leaves to remain lying in autumn, especially if in a thick layer, as they can cause damage to the grass when they rot. They should be raked up and put onto the compost heap to make humus.

TRIMMING LAWN EDGES

Left—Using long-handled edging shears. The regular use of this tool ensures a neat and tidy appearance and prevents grass from encroaching on to the flower bed or border.

Right—Trimming edges with a "half moon", or edging tool. Do not take off more than an inch or so at a time. Tidy edges improve the appearance of both lawn and flower beds.

Left—With a product called Lawn Edge (made from aluminium alloy) set upright on the edge, trimming with edging shears is all that is required for maintaining the edge and preventing breaking.

Right—A Jalo Lawn Edger can be used for trimming edges. For efficient working it is essential that the edges be kept vertical with the edging tool.

FERTILISING A LAWN

Right—Applying a fertiliser mixture in autumn after first marking off a strip one yard wide. A suitable mixture is two parts superphosphate, one part sulphate of ammonia and one part sulphate of potash; this should be applied at four oz. per sq. yd. *Below*—Brushing in a top-dressing of soil and peat—half of each—in autumn. Such a dressing may follow spiking, filling in the holes. It improves rooting and growth generally.

Above—For a large lawn area, a Quillot may be used to apply fertiliser dressings. This machine is supplied with different rollers for distributing different amounts. Most dressings can be applied by going over the lawn twice or three times. *Left*—Where the soil is heavy and the lawn tends to lie wet on the surface, a dressing of coarse sand is of benefit. This can be applied at the rate of $\frac{1}{4}$ to $\frac{1}{2}$ lb. per sq. yd and may follow spiking.

Right—Applying a lawn weed killer to yard-wide strips. Follow makers' directions carefully as to rate of application and always apply on a calm day to prevent any danger of drifting on to cultivated plants, or damage will result.

WEED CONTROL

Left — One method of dealing with broad-leaved weeds and moss is to use lawn sand, which should be applied at 4 oz. per sq. yd. on a fine dry day in spring or early summer.

Left—The effect of a lawn weed killer on plantains. The effect on other broad-leaved weeds is similar. After curling and twisting of the foliage, the plants die. Grass is unharmed.

Right—Spot treatment of individual weeds by using a special wax stock impregnated with lawn weed killer—the same type of lawn weed killer as that often applied by spray. This method of application avoids any danger of drift.

TYPES OF MOWERS—I

Below—A side-wheel mower with grass box and rear plate removed. Regular adjustment and close attention to oiling and maintenance are essential for best results. This is the cheapest type of lawn mower in general use.

Above—A roller mower. This popular type is efficient for general purposes and is useful for cutting over the edges of a lawn.

Below—A motor mower being used on a larger area, where the size of the lawn justifies the expenditure. It gives quick, labour-saving mowing, and can be easily handled by most women.

Above—A rotary mower with power-driven blades (cutter bars). With this type of machine grass cuttings are left on the surface or can be collected into a sack attached to the side of the handle. Mowers of this kind can cut long grass —in orchards, for example—with no effort.

TYPES OF MOWERS—2

Left—A rotary mower which works on a cushion of air and is especially useful for cutting grass under bushes and on sloping ground.

Right—A battery mower. The battery can be recharged with a trickle charger, and will work for about four hours on one charge.

Left—An electrically driven rotary cutter for small areas. The power unit is one also used for many other operations in home and garden, and is linked to the nearest power point with heavy cable. There are also cylinder mowers powered from the mains electricity supply.

Right—A rotary mower fitted with seat, used for small paddocks, grass orchards and similar areas of rough grass. This is an invention that has come from America, and is now being used by clubs in this country.

ANCILLARY MOWING EQUIPMENT

Right — A roller fitted with spikes for lawn aeration. This type of equipment is particularly useful for improving both aeration and drainage in a lawn. It is best used in autumn. *Below*— A hand-operated lawn aerator, suitable for smaller areas. Improved aeration is often one of the first operations to consider in a neglected lawn.

Above—The attachment shown here, for use with the Gardenmaster, is a rotary scarifier, and is particularly useful where moss is present. *Left*—An Allen Lawn Sweeper gathering leaves. This equipment can also be used for gathering up cut grass where a rotary mower has been used.

SETTING MOWERS

Below— The lower the front roller is set, the higher the cut will be. At the beginning of the season it is advisable only to top the grass, and to do this the roller should be in the lowest position, as here.

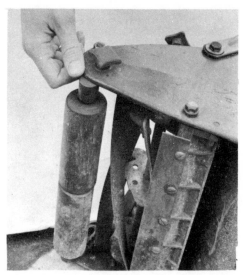

Above—As the season progresses, the front roller should be raised to give a closer cut and a neater appearance to the lawn.

Below—Whenever the roller is adjusted it is essential that the side locking nuts be firmly tightened. Slipping of the nuts will cause uneven cutting.

Above—Some rotary cutters have four wheels, which raise or lower in pairs. In the machine shown here, a centre wing nut controls front and back rollers, lifting or dropping the rotary cutters according to the height of cut required.

PLANTING A BUSH ROSE—I

Left—Bushes may arrive bundled in sacking, roots protected with straw. In cold, frosty weather, a bundle can be left unpacked in a shed or garage for 1–2 weeks without harm.

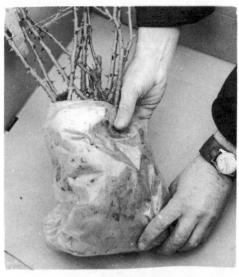

Right—Bushes may also arrive in a stout polythene bag. Unpack bushes purchased in a can or container from garden centres as soon as possible and heel them in (see opposite page).

Left above—Bushes received later in the season may be already pruned and ready for planting. *Left below*—Before planting, pull off any buds on the roots below the point of budding. If left, these give rise to undesirable sucker growths.

Right—Dip the roots in a bucket of water before planting. Leave the roots in water for 3–4 hours if they are dry.

PLANTING A BUSH ROSE—2

Below—Bushes should be "heeled in" (planted temporarily) when received, if the site is not ready. They can stay heeled in for several weeks if necessary. Label all bushes.

Above—Take out a planting hole large enough to accommodate the roots without their being cramped, i.e. so that they can be spread out evenly.

Below—Set the bush in the centre of the hole, and at such a depth that the "union" (point of budding) will not be covered by soil.

Above—Start to fill in with soil, spreading evenly over the exposed roots. Lift the bush a few inches once or twice to settle the soil around and under the roots.

PLANTING A BUSH ROSE—3

Left—When about half the required amount of soil has been filled in, hold the branches upright and firm around the hole.

Right—Firm the soil evenly by treading. Never plant when the soil is sticky.

Left—After firming, add more soil to give the required depth of planting and firm again evenly.

Right—When planting is completed, the budding point should be just below the soil level.

PLANTING A STANDARD ROSE

Below—Set the stake firmly in place on the south-west side of the tree. Stand the tree in the planting hole with roots spread out.

Above—Firm the soil evenly as planting proceeds. Plant the tree at its previous depth, which may be determined by the soil mark at the base of the main stem.

Below—Tie the tree securely to the top of the stake, using thick twine or plastic tree ties. Note the position of the top of the stake in relation to the base of the branches.

Above—Label each tree clearly at the time of planting, or before the name tag becomes unreadable.

FEEDING ROSES

Left—Apply a dressing of a general fertiliser in early spring before the usual mulch is put on. A suitable mixture is two parts bone meal, one part hoof and horn and one part sulphate of potash at 4 oz. per sq. yd.

Right—Apply manure mulch as a top-dressing in spring, and later on as an aid to moisture retention. Compost may be used as an alternative to manure.

Left—A mulch being applied in early summer as an aid to moisture retention. Lawn mowings may be used, put down in weekly layers through the summer.

Right—Applying a feed in summer. This can be equal parts of hoof and horn and sulphate of potash, at 2 oz. per sq. yd. A proprietary rose fertiliser can be used at maker's directions.

SPRAYING AND DUSTING

Above left— Spraying with an insecticide in summer against greenfly. Spray at the first signs of attack and repeat as necessary. *Above right*—When spring cleaning the rose bed, ensure that all dead leaves are gathered up and burnt, as these hold the spores of black spot.

Above—Spraying in early spring against black spot. A Captan fungicide may be used for this purpose; soil as well as bushes should be treated. *Left*—Dusting with Karathene against mildew with a small rotary dustblower. It is best to dust at the first sign of attack; do not wait until mildew is well advanced before taking control measures.

SOME CULTURAL TIPS

Below—With hybrid tea roses, do not leave buds in clusters of three where large blooms are required.

Above—Retain the central bud and cut out the two smaller buds at the sides cleanly.

Below—Cut off the dead flower heads and seed pod "hips" each week. Cut back to a sound bud, from which the next flowers will come.

Above—Paving slabs are good aids to window cleaning and prevent undue firming of the soil beneath windows.

BASIC PRUNING OF ROSES

Left—Remove thin, short growths and dead or broken shoots.

Right—Take out any crossing branches, aiming at keeping the centre of the bush open.

Left—Take out or cut back to a suitable length any badly placed shoots.

Right—When these basic points have been attended to, commence pruning the main branches.

PRUNING MAIN BRANCHES

Right—A strong growing floribunda rose bush after basic pruning.

Left—Shorten back main branches to about half way. A sharp knife or pair of sécateurs is essential.

Right—Prune each of the main branches to an outward pointing bud.

Left—Pruning completed.

SOME TIPS ON ROSE PRUNING

Left—Ends of young growths on roses are often flabby and soft. If finger pressure shows that shoots are in this condition, i.e. unripened, cut back to firm tissue. *Below*—The only correct pruning cut here is on the extreme right. All the others are incorrect.

Below left—When a pruning cut is made too high above a bud, a "snag" is left and disease may enter to cause a rotting back, as shown here. *Below right*—Confusion may arise between a wood bud and a flower bud. A wood bud is shown here. If a shoot is cut back to just above such a bud, it will normally develop a new shoot.

PRUNING A YOUNG FLORIBUNDA

Left—First take out weak and dead wood shoots, cutting out the wood cleanly from the base or point of origin.

Right—The main framework branches ready for pruning.

Left—Cut branches back to about half way or slightly less if the bush is very strong, slightly more if weak growing. Cut to an outward pointing bud.

Right—Pruning completed.

PRUNING A NEWLY
PLANTED BUSH
Below — Hybrid teas and floribundas should be pruned immediately after planting.

Above—Remove thin, weak growths cleanly from the base.

Below—Cut back each main shoot to just above a bud, leaving two or three buds on the remaining part of the shoot.

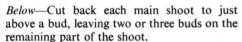

Above—Pruning completed. Each shoot is cut back to an outward pointing bud.

PRUNING AN OLD HYBRID TEA—I

Left — A bush before pruning.

Right—Remove thin, weak shoots to leave the main strong growing branches. Cut away all dead wood cleanly.

Left—The main branches after removal of thin, weak shoots.

Right—Prune back the main branches to a half or a third of their growth. The extent of pruning depends on the variety and condition of the bush. A neglected bush should be pruned severely, as illustrated here.

PRUNING AN OLD HYBRID TEA—2

Below—When pruning is nearly completed check whether any "stubs" can be removed, such as that on the right of this bush.

Above—Remove the stub cleanly and as low down as possible. Use a large sharp knife or sécateurs.

Below—Next, check whether any other older stubs can be taken out, such as the one in the foreground on the right.

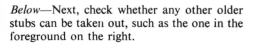

Above—Pruning completed. This type of pruning is of benefit on an old bush, encouraging strong new growth from the base.

PRUNING A STANDARD ROSE

Left—Prune on the same principles as a bush rose, first taking out any thin twiggy or crossing shoots. These should be removed flush with the branch from which they arise.

Right—After the thin twiggy growths and the crossing shoots have been removed, shorten back the main branches to about half way, always cutting to an outward pointing bud.

Left—Pruning completed. This type of pruning aims at keeping the centre of the head open, and an outward pointing branch formation. This gives balanced growth and a well shaped head.

Right—Retain young, strong shoots for tying full length to the supports. If there are several of these, cut out the weakest ones.

Right—Tying new growths back into place, all the older stems having been removed cleanly to soil level.

PRUNING A RAMBLER ROSE

Left—Prune in autumn. Release all ties and cut out old stems which have flowered, at soil level. The best flowers are produced on young shoots.

Left—If there are few young growths, retain the old stems, but shorten back all the laterals (side growths) to two or three buds.

PRUNING A CLIMBING ROSE

Left—Cut back newly planted climbing roses to 2 ft in height to a sound bud. The resulting growth after one season is shown here: note the new shoots from the base.

Right—Tie back main growths to the supporting post. As these growths will be retained for some years, arrange them to give the best display.

Left—Normal yearly pruning consists of shortening back the laterals on the main growths to leave two or three buds, from which the flowers are produced.

Right—Cut out an old stem with a saw each year as base shoots are produced.

THE HERBACEOUS BORDER

Left—A well-planned, mixed herbaceous border provides a wide range of colour over a long period from early summer to late autumn.

Right—The background (here a tall fence) plays an important part, not only showing up colours but also providing shelter.

Left—An evergreen hedge makes a good background, being excellent both for setting off colours and as a wind-break.

Right—An "island" border set in a lawn enables the plants to be seen from all sides. The informal shape is generally more attractive than the formal.

PLANTING A HERBACEOUS
BORDER—I *Left*—Herbaceous plants are best planted in autumn. Heel them in if they cannot be planted. Do not plant when the soil is wet.

Right—Mark out the site for each plant. For a large border, use groups of two or three instead of single plants.

Left—Plants being laid out 18 in. apart on a site. Plan the layout beforehand so that heights, colours and times of flowering are balanced to give a display for as long as possible.

Right—An alternative layout is four plants to a square yard. This is an average spacing for a mixed batch of plants.

PLANTING A HERBACEOUS BORDER—2

Below—Two different types of herbaceous plant, one with spreading fibrous roots and the other with a thick, long main root system.

Above—Use a spade to plant deep-rooted subjects in order to obtain the necessary depth.

Below—For smaller plants a trowel may be used. It is important to spread the roots in the planting hole so that they are not cramped.

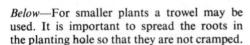

Above—Set plants singly at 18-in. spacing and make sure that all are planted firmly. Set divided plants at their previous depth.

LABELLING

Left—Correct labelling adds to the pleasure of a herbaceous border, especially where named varieties have been purchased. If wooden labels are used, they should be painted and written on in black "garden" pencil.

Right—Labels on short legs are useful for border work, and should be set in place as soon as possible, either at planting time or shortly afterwards. Paper labels attached to the stems of purchased plants should be replaced before they rot.

Left—The Dymo Label-maker produces sticky labels in a variety of colours by a simple letter dialling system.

THE HERBACEOUS BORDER IN SPRING—I

Left— Where slug damage is likely, protect the new shoots as soon as they appear. Delphiniums and pyrethrums are especially prone to attack, and slug bait pellets should be placed in position before damage occurs.

Right—An alternative or extra measure of protection is to place a ring of soot around each clump of plants. Ashes may be used if soot is not available.

Left—After the above work has been completed, fork between the plants to remove footmarks. Where possible, do as much general tidying up as practicable in autumn, including a light forking through, as pressure of other work in spring may mean that the herbaceous border suffers.

THE HERBACEOUS BORDER IN SPRING—2

Right—A mulch of peat or compost, or well-rotted farm-yard manure, is of especial benefit on light sandy soil. It should be spread evenly between the clumps of plants. *Below*—A top-dressing of a proprietary complete fertiliser at 3 oz. per sq. yd should be applied evenly between the plants in spring when growth starts, and hoed into the top few inches of soil.

Above—A shallow forking with a short-tined or small border fork keeps down weeds, prevents the surface soil from setting hard, and leaves the border tidy for the new season. *Left*—When border plants have spread and are growing too close together, cut and lift away with a trowel the unwanted part of each clump.

THINNING SHOOTS

Left—Subjects like delphiniums, which make tall growths and bold spikes, give the best display when three or four spikes are allowed to develop on each clump. A well-established clump may have twelve shoots, and if all are left, quality of flower and length of spike suffer. *Below*— Thin the shoots when 4 in. high to leave three or four of the best spikes to each clump. The shoots which are removed can be used as cuttings.

Below left—A clump of Michaelmas daisies with about twenty shoots before thinning. *Below right*—Thin Michaelmas daisies when the new shoots are about 4 in. high by cutting away unwanted growths cleanly with a sharp knife. Up to half the number of shoots may be removed, leaving the remainder evenly spaced.

STAKING

Left—Tall plants need support. A large clump (2 ft or so across) may be supported by string tied once or twice round equally spaced 4–5 ft canes.

Right—Short plants (up to 18 in. in height), such as those shown in the foreground, need not be staked.

Left—Tall plants like delphiniums may be supported by a 5–6-ft stake to each clump. Leave a space of $\frac{1}{2}$ in. between stake and stem after tying, and tie in each main stem separately.

Right—Herbaceous plants with bushy growth 2 ft or so in height are best supported with twiggy pea sticks about two-thirds of the ultimate height of the plants. Set this in place when the plant growth is 1 ft in height.

MAINTENANCE OF THE HERBACEOUS BORDER

Left—Heads of dead flowers should be taken off regularly. This helps to keep a continuity of flowering in many plants. Remove old flower stalks as well as faded flowers.

Right—One of the chief pests of herbaceous border plants is green-fly. Other aphids may also attack certain plants, and some caterpillar pests can be troublesome. Spray any plant attacked with a derris or pyrethrum preparation at the first signs of attack.

Left—The need for adequate staking is easily seen here. Tall subjects can easily be damaged by high wind, and give a very bedraggled appearance to a border, spoiling what would otherwise be a perfect display.

THE HERBACEOUS BORDER IN AUTUMN

Below—Take out canes and stakes and store them in a dry place over winter. Make sure that labels are not displaced.

Above—Cut down dead stems to near soil level in autumn or early winter. In cold or exposed areas this may be delayed until spring for extra protection; tall stems should then be reduced by half in autumn

Below—Cut off dead foliage with shears where leaves are thick and matted and where cutting with a knife or sécateurs would be a lengthy job.

Above—When cutting back the dead stems in spring, take care not to damage the new buds. Cut out the old growths to soil level. The dead stems can be composted: cut into short lengths first to aid rotting down.

SPRING BEDDING—1

Most spring flowering plants are best planted in autumn. *Left*—After clearing away spent summer flowering plants and firming where necessary, apply a dressing of complete fertiliser at 4 oz. per sq. yd, preferably immediately before planting.

Right—Work the dressing into the top few inches of the bed with an iron rake.

Left—Mark out the bed with shallow drills 9 in. apart. If this is done each way, the crossing points become the positions for plants. A plank should be used to stand on throughout.

Right—Polyanthus should be planted down to the level of the lowest leaves. Remove any low yellow foliage.

Right—Polyanthus in mixed colours and myosotis are a popular choice. Plant firmly in each case.

SPRING BEDDING—2

Left—Stand on a plank while planting. This prevents uneven consolidation from footprints. Here a bed of myosotis (Forget-me-not) is being planted.

Left—Clumps of polyanthus being laid out in position ready for planting. These subjects make a good display by themselves.

SPRING BEDDING—3

Left—Myosotis can be planted by itself or in combination with tulips, the blue flowers making a sharp contrast with red and yellow tulips.

Right—Pansies make a colourful display by themselves where low growing subjects are required, or a colourful edging to other subjects.

Left—Polyanthus, pansies and wallflowers make a colourful combination. Pansies can be planted either as an edging or mixed in with the other subjects.

Right—Siberian wallflower and Canterbury Bell are another good planting combination. A narrow border alongside a path lends itself well to a spring display.

Right—Siberian wallflower makes a brilliant show of colour. Its orange flowers make a good groundwork for red or pink tulips.

SPRING BEDDING—4

Left—Canterbury Bell, being taller than most spring bedding subjects, is best planted in a bed by itself but is also suitable for a mixed display.

Left—Brompton stock is not fully hardy in all areas, and a severe frost may kill some of the plants. It is best to keep a few plants in reserve to make good any losses.

Right—Sweet William is best planted in a bed by itself, as it flowers later than most other spring flowering plants. It is very free flowering; a wide range of red and pink shades is very suitable for a late spring display.

SPRING BEDDING—5: PLANTING WALLFLOWERS

Left—Mark out shallow drills at 9-in. spacing in both directions and lay out the plants at the intersections of the squares.

Right—Well-branched plants give the best display. If young plants are stopped when 4–5 in. high, they "break" (branch out) to give bushy plants like the one on the left.

Left—When planting, set the plants at the level of the lowest side shoots. Take out a hole large and deep enough to take roots without cramping. It is often necessary to re-firm after a frost.

Right—During a severe winter some plants may suffer and spoil the display if left. Always keep a few plants in reserve to make good losses.

SPRING BEDDING—6

Left—Tulip bulbs being planted with myosotis. Plant 9 in. apart and 4 in. deep. Pink varieties blend well with the blue of myosotis.

Right—When planting is completed, hoe through lightly between the plants or prick the surface of the bed lightly with a small border fork.

Left—A bed with planting completed and surface soil hoed. No further attention will be needed until early spring.

SPRING BEDDING—7: MAINTENANCE

Left—Tidy lawn edges set off a bed of spring flowering subjects like polyanthus. Clip the grass and weed the bed regularly.

Right—Remove the faded flower heads from pansies to ensure a longer display of bloom. Pansies blend well with other spring flowering subjects such as myosotis, Siberian wallflower and polyanthus.

Left—Remove dead flower heads from polyanthus—unless seed is being saved—lift the plants after flowering and replant them in a semi-shaded site. Plants may be divided at this stage.

SUMMER BEDDING—I

Left—Fork through the bed in mid-May to obtain a good tilth and tread the bed evenly. Plants dislike loose ground, especially where the soil is light.

Right—Apply a dressing of a proprietary general fertiliser at 4 oz. per sq. yd, or use a mixture of three parts bone meal, one part sulphate of ammonia and one part sulphate of potash at 4 oz. per sq. yd.

Left—Marking out for planting. This type of marker can be adjusted to mark at different intervals.

Right—Another method of marking out is to use a planting board. Plant at intersections of lines or in the centre of each square.

Right—Stake and tie immediately after planting so as to cause minimum disturbance of the bed.

SUMMER BEDDING—2

Left—Fuchsias or other tall plants spaced at intervals along the centre of the bed help to relieve the "flatness" of a bed containing a single variety.

Left—To prevent damage to grass edges, work wherever possible from a plank.

Right—After working on grass verges, keep the grass fresh by giving it a good brushing with a birch broom.

SUMMER BEDDING—3

Left—Before removing plants from a box, give them a good soaking with a rosed can to ensure that the soil will adhere to the roots and not fall away when handled.

Right—After allowing the box to drain, tap first one end and then one side on the floor to loosen the roots adhering to the bottom and sides.

Left—Carefully remove one side of the box without damaging it—it can be replaced after the plants have been removed.

Right—Hold the box each side and shake the contents out intact on to a flat surface ready for dividing up.

SUMMER BEDDING—4

Below—Cut away a single line of plants. Individual plants can then be cut out with a solid soil square ensuring minimum root disturbance and little or no check when planted.

Above—Set the plants so that they are slightly deeper than they were previously. Take out a hole large enough to accommodate the roots without cramping.

Below—Firm the soil lightly around each plant. Good summer bedding plants are antirrhinum, ten week stock, nemesia, aster, nicotiana and mesembryanthemum. Plant in mid-May.

Above—After planting, water the plants carefully, especially in dry weather. If planted in dull weather following rain, they will grow with a minimum of check.

PLANTING FROM POTS

Left—Strip off the pots, unless roots have developed into the pot material, in which case they can be left and planted intact. Some popular pot-grown summer plants are petunia, salvia and geranium.

Right—When planting geraniums from clay pots, knock the plants out carefully and plant fairly firmly, so that the top of the ball of soil is covered by about 2 in. of new soil.

Left—An edging of lobelia or alyssum, or both, makes a good finish to any summer bedding display. Plant carefully and leave about 6 in. between plant and edge of bed.

PLANTING DAHLIA TUBERS

Below—Dormant tubers that have been stored through winter should be planted out in late May. The new growth will take a fortnight or so to come through.

Above—Cover the tubers with 3–4 in. of soil.

Below—Tubers started in trays or boxes in the greenhouse are often too large to be planted by themselves.

Above—Tubers which are too large can be divided with a sharp knife. Ensure that each piece has a fair share of roots.

PLANTING DAHLIAS FROM POTS—1

Left—Holes should be large enough to take soil balls without disturbance of roots. Take out each planting hole separately in a prepared bed.

Right—Place a forkful of compost, or better, well-rotted manure, at the bottom of each hole and mix it in.

Left—To remove a plant from a clay pot, place the fingers across the top of the pot with the plant between them, and up-end the pot.

Right—Give the rim a sharp tap on the handle of a spade, and the pot will then lift off without damage to the roots.

PLANTING DAHLIAS FROM POTS—2

Below—Remove any crocks from the base of the ball of soil. Ease the pieces out carefully so as to prevent damage to roots.

Above—Plant so that the top of the ball is covered with 1 in. of soil.

Below—In exposed positions, insert a cane or stake. This is best done immediately after planting, so that roots are not damaged.

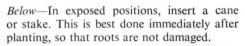

Above—Dahlia plants are very susceptible to damage from wind, and should be tied to the support with a couple of loops of garden string.

ESTABLISHED DAHLIAS

Below—When free growth starts, feed with a proprietary complete fertiliser at 4 oz. per sq. yd, or use 2 parts bone meal, 1 part hoof and horn, 1 part sulphate of potash at 4 oz. per sq. yd.

Above—Hoe in the top-dressing with a short-handled hoe. Hold back the young growth with one hand while working the dressing in where it will do most good.

Below—Hoe regularly to keep down weeds and to keep the soil open, and also before applying a top-dressing.

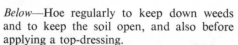

Above—A mulch of well-rotted manure or garden compost is of benefit, especially on a light, sandy soil. Place in position all round and between the plants to a depth of 2–3 in.

ANTI-PEST MEASURES

Left—Young dahlias are soft and therefore very vulnerable to attack from slugs and snails. At planting time scatter a few slug pellets around each plant.

Right—At a later date the plants may be attacked by aphides and caterpillars. Dust with derris at regular intervals at the first signs of damage.

Left—Earwigs are the greatest menace to blooms and buds, many blooms being spoilt because of eaten petals. Traps can be made from small pots and hay or straw.

Right—Place a little hay or straw at the bottom of a small pot and place the pot over a stake. Examine the trap daily and destroy the earwigs found.

DISBUDDING DAHLIAS

Above left—If no disbudding or shoot thinning is done, flowers will be small. They are usually formed in threes.   *Above centre*—For larger blooms, take out the side buds and leave the central one at the stage shown here or a little earlier. *Above right*—If extra long stems and exhibition flowers are required remove the two side shoots below the flower bud.

Above—Prompt attention is essential if the bud left is to develop perfectly. Buds can be removed quite easily with the finger and thumb at the stage shown here.   *Left*—There is little point in removing side flower stems at this stage, as the buds are on the point of opening.

Right—By re-staking in this way no damage will be caused to the tubers. Tie in the tall growth and any new lower shoots. Stems are very brittle and easily damaged by wind.

RE-STAKING AND REMOVING SEED HEADS

Left—Strong growing plants will often require another stake as the season progresses. When such extra staking is required, work the new support into the ground close to the old one.

Left—Removal of spent flowers to ensure continuous bloom should be a regular job, especially with bedding dahlias. Care should be taken to distinguish between flower buds and seed heads.

Right—The flower bud is on the left. It is smaller than the seed head of the spent flower on the right and has a flat end.

LIFTING DAHLIAS

Above left—Dahlias are among the first plants in the garden to become blackened by frost. When this happens, they should be lifted and the stems cut back to leave 6–9 in. *Above right*— Lift each plant carefully with a fork, damaging the tubers as little as possible. Wash off the surplus soil and allow to dry.

Above—Each root should have its label securely tied to the length of stem left, so that when the tubers are boxed it can be easily read. *Left*—Tubers stored in boxes are best placed on a layer of fine weathered cinders or peat. First dust with flowers of sulphur as a precaution against mildew, then work a little of the cinders or peat between and over the roots.

PLANTING CHRYSANTHEMUMS

Left—Chrysanthemums do not require deep planting. Take out a planting hole large enough to take the soil ball without cramping. *Below*—After setting the plant in position, move the soil in around the plant and firm gently with the trowel handle.

Below left—On completion of planting, set a stake by each plant and make the first tie. Four-foot canes pushed about 1 ft into the ground are ideal. *Below right*—Spray regularly with an insecticide suitable for chrysanthemum pests. Ensure that both tops and undersides of leaves are well covered. Spray every 7 to 10 days.

Right—Stopping encourages side growths. The number of side growths which are retained depends on whether large, small or medium-sized blooms are required. For a general display five or six may be kept.

STOPPING AND DISBUDDING CHRYSANTHEMUMS
Left—When early flowering outdoor varieties are 7–8 in. high, they can be "stopped". Nip off about 1 in. at the growing point back to a leaf.

Right—Unwanted side growths from below the bud must also be removed, and are best taken out carefully when small. Remove such side growths from the whole length of stem beneath the flower bud.

Left—For large blooms, where sprays of flowers are not wanted, only the terminal bud of each stem should be allowed to remain. Remove other buds around this bud when small.

TYING AND SUPPORTING CHRYSANTHEMUMS

Left—When tying a young chrysanthemum to the stake, leave a finger-width's space between stake and stem.

Right—As the stems grow, the space between shoots and stake should be increased to enable the flower to form without touching the stake.

Left—Rain collecting in the crown of the bloom, causing petals to go brown and mildewy, can easily bring much careful work to ruin.

Right—So can damage by earwigs if vigilance is relaxed. Petals are eaten away and made ragged.

PROTECTING CHRYSANTHEMUM BLOOMS

Left—In late summer and early autumn, cover the whole plant with a polythene bag for protection against wind and rain.

Right—Individual blooms can be protected by a sheet of greaseproof paper about 15 in. square.

Left—Fold the sheet of greaseproof paper over and secure it to the stem at a point beneath the bloom. A snap-type clothes peg may be used for this purpose.

Right—When a bed of chrysanthemums is grown for showing, a temporary structure made from stout stakes and reinforced polythene makes a good shelter.

CHRYSANTHEMUMS IN WINTER

Left—Where plants are grown in ground which is wanted for spring flowering subjects, lift and store the stools in boxes for the winter.

Right—Whether the plants are left or lifted, the spent top growth must be cut down and burnt In spring fresh growth will appear.

Left—It is unwise to leave large clumps to grow on; these should be lifted and divided. Single pieces with roots—sometimes called "Irishman's cuttings"—are usually easy to detach.

Right—With roots stored in boxes, it will often be found that young growth in the early part of the year is marked by wandering white tunnels; this is a leaf miner. Spray with BHC.

PLANTING CARNATIONS

Left—Young plants are usually sold in 3-in. pots, and they may be raised in pots of this size. Plant in spring in well-prepared soil in a sunny position.

Right—Take out a hole slightly larger than the ball of soil and add some sand to the base if the soil is heavy. Good drainage is essential.

Left—Take the plant from its pot with care, so that the ball of soil remains intact. It can be removed by tapping the rim on the corner of a hard surface.

Right—Plant and firm the soil evenly all round. This ensures that the plant will become established, and make sturdy growth.

"STOPPING" CARNATIONS

Below—When young plants have started to grow after being planted out, they should be "stopped".

Above—Nip off about an inch of the growing tip.

Below—A plant after stopping. Make sure that the portion removed is nipped off cleanly.

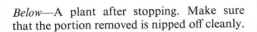

Above—After stopping, the plant will develop side growths—usually about three or four. This ensures a bushy plant with plenty of flowering stems.

ESTABLISHED CARNATIONS

Left– As the young plants become established, hoe the soil shallowly between them, taking care not to damage the surface roots.

Right—Give each plant a short cane as support and tie in the new growths securely. Unsupported plants tend to flop and become straggly.

Left—Short bushy pea sticks may also be used as supporting material. They tend to be hidden by the foliage and do not detract from the flowering display.

Right—A top-dressing of 1–2 in. of a mixture of two parts good loam, two parts sand and one part limestone chippings will give good results.

"STOPPING" SWEET PEAS

Below—Remove about half an inch below the growing point back to a leaf when the plant is 4 in. high.

Above—After stopping, one, two or three strong shoots will develop. Any weak shoots which result should be completely removed.

Below—Retain the two best "breaks" (new growths) and train them to the same cane. If several plants with two breaks are being grown, allow wider spacing between them when planting.

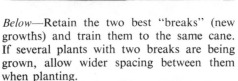

Above—When growing for show, plants with single shoots at 12–14-in. spacing will give best results.

Right—Take out a planting hole large enough to accommodate the roots without cramping.

PLANTING SWEET PEAS

Left—Young plants, grown in 3- or $3\frac{1}{2}$-in. pots, can be planted out of doors in late March. If they have been raised under glass or in frames, harden them off well before planting.

Left—Plant fairly firmly. Water in dry spells to encourage early establishment.

Right—Bushy pea sticks set in place at planting time or shortly afterwards give protection from cold winds.

SWEET PEAS AFTER PLANTING

Below—Where plants are grown on a single stem, careful tying is essential. Wire rings, which can be purchased from most garden sundries shops, provide a quick and easy method.

Above—Remove all tendrils as they develop, otherwise these may become entangled with flower stems. Daily attention is needed when plants are growing strongly.

Below—Remove all side growths from the axils of the leaves when small. This should be done cleanly with a sharp knife or a small pair of scissors.

Above—The first flowers borne are usually very small and of poor quality, and should be removed. This should be done until the plants are about 4 ft high.

Right—Release the plants from the canes when they reach the top, lay them down flat and then re-train them up canes further along. Take care not to kink the stems when doing this work.

Right—Use tripods of canes when cut blooms are grown, leaving sufficient room between the canes to enable the blooms to be cut.

SWEET PEAS—METHODS OF SUPPORT

Left—For growing top quality blooms use 8-ft or taller canes, especially where plants are trained as single stems. Tie the canes to wires which should be fixed to stout posts.

Left—String netting is an alternative method of support. Fix this to a wire at the top and bottom.

PLANTING BULBS

Above left—Narcissi and daffodils are among the most popular bulbs for spring flowering. Plant in the autumn, 5 in. deep on light soils and 4 in. on heavy.

Above right—A bulb planter may be used when planting a large number of bulbs. This removes a ball of soil so that bulbs can be set in position.

Above—Narcissi give the best display when planted in a bold group. Set the bulbs 4–5 in. apart beneath a tree or around shrubs.

Right—For naturalising in grass, lift and roll back a square of turf. Set the bulbs about 3 in. deep and 6 in. apart. Replace turf and tread firm.

STORING NARCISSI AND DAFFODILS

Below—After flowering has finished, gather the foliage together and tie into a knot. This will allow the bulbs to develop fully, improving next season's flower display.

Above—An alternative method, where the foliage is short, is to bend it over and secure with a rubber band.

Below—If the bulbs are lifted after flowering, store them in dry, cool conditions. This should not be done until the foliage has died down naturally.

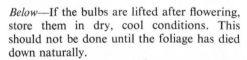

Above—Sort over the bulbs prior to replanting and discard any which are damaged or diseased. Small bulbs can be planted separately to grow on to flowering size.

PLANTING GLADIOLI

Left—Set the corms 3 in. deep, with a little sand at the base of each planting hole, in clumps of three to five for a good display.

Right—Plant the corms 4 in. apart in rows 6 in. apart where a quantity is required for cut flower purposes.

Left—If the plants are in a row or narrow bed support may be given by canes and string. Two sets of string are required, at 1 ft and 2 ft from soil level.

Right—Single plants of a tall variety are best staked separately, especially if in an exposed position. Use a 4-ft cane for each plant.

STORING GLADIOLUS CORMS

Left—As soon as the flowers have faded cut away the old flower stalks and lift the corms with the foliage. Tie into convenient bundles for drying.

Below left—The small cormlets (often called "spawn" or "peas") at the base of the large hard corm can be saved and planted in the spring. They will need two or three years' growth to reach flowering size.

Above right—Remove all the remains of dead foliage and store only the sound corms in a cool, dry place. Keep in frost-proof conditions during the winter.

Right—After removing the top growth, work off any loose skin and the remains of the old roots from the base before packing away.

TULIPS AND HYACINTHS

Above left—Plant tulips in the autumn and cover to a depth of 4 in. in a light soil and 3 in. in a heavy soil.

Above right—Plant hyacinths in the autumn so that the top of each bulb is covered to a depth of 5 in.—4 in. in heavy soil. Place some sand in the bottom of the planting hole.

Above—Lift the bulbs after flowering and plant temporarily in a shallow trench until the foliage dies down naturally. Then lift and store the bulbs.

Right—In autumn the small offsets at the sides of each main bulb should be detached when dry and planted separately to grow on.

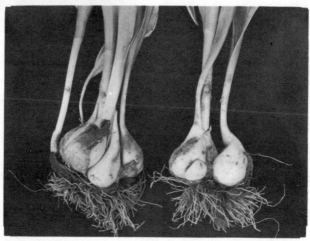

MUSCARI, CROCUS AND LILIES

Left—Plant muscari in groups of six to nine, setting the bulbs 4 in. apart and covering them to a depth of 3 in. These plants are useful for providing colour in the spring.

Right—Crocus make an early display of colour. Set the corms in bold groups 3–4 in. apart, and cover to a depth of 2–3 in.

Left—Lift long-established clumps of crocus at three- to four-year intervals and separate the corms when the foliage has died down. Store the corms in a cool place until planting time in early autumn.

Right—Lilies are best planted in groups of four to six in order to give a pleasing display quickly. Depth of planting, usually 4–6 in., depends upon variety.

PREPARING A TUB FOR PLANTING

Below—Tubs for planting are available in various sizes. As the drainage is of the utmost importance, check that the holes are clear.

Above—To prevent the drainage holes becoming blocked with soil, cover them inside the barrel with large pieces of crock. This will also stop worms from working their way in.

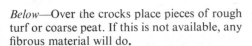

Below—Over the crocks place pieces of rough turf or coarse peat. If this is not available, any fibrous material will do.

Above—Put the rough turf in to a depth of 6 in. This will also hold moisture and prevent the barrel from drying out too quickly.

FILLING A TUB WITH SOIL

Left—Fill the tub with compost of four parts loam to one part each of peat and sand. To each bucketful of this mixture add a handful of a general fertiliser.

Right—Firm the compost two or three times while filling the tub. Leave a 2–3 in. space at the top for watering.

Left—Geraniums can be used with colourful effect. Plant them firmly and close together to give a lasting display. If red flowers are used, bear in mind the colour of the tub in which they stand.

PLANTING IN A TUB

Right—If using geraniums in whalehide pots, remove the pot material before planting. Do not disturb the roots more than necessary.

Left—Where plants in flower can be used, an instant effect is obtained. Do not plant tender subjects until danger of frost has passed.

Right—Water in immediately after planting, paying close attention to this point in summer months. Plants will benefit from a weekly feed with a liquid fertiliser.

PLANTING IN A TROUGH

Left—Concrete troughs are cast with a number of small holes in the bottom for drainage. Cover these with crocks before placing a layer of rough turf over the bottom.

Right—Planting in progress, using large clumps of poly-anthus. This can be done in autumn or spring. Bulbs can be planted in autumn to give added colour and blend well with myosotis.

Left—Plants like polyanthus are best grown in a bed and planted in the trough 2–3 weeks before flowering. Spring-flowering bulbs should be planted in the autumn.

Right—Position the plants before finally planting to obtain the best effect.

SUMMER FLOWERS IN A WINDOW BOX

Left — Fill the box with compost. Add a dressing of general fertiliser and work it into the top few inches of compost.

Left—When tuberous begonias are used as the main feature set them at the front of the box. A trailing variety will give a good contrast.

Right—As an alternative arrangement, use geraniums (zonal pelargoniums) as the main feature, with an ivy leaf variety to trail down the front of the box.

Right—Line the basket to halfway up the wire with perforated polythene and moss, or moss alone.

Right—Half fill the basket with compost. J.I.P. 1 is very suitable, or use a mixture of three parts loam, two parts peat and one part sand. Damp the compost before filling.

HANGING BASKETS— PREPARING TO PLANT

Left—A 10-in. wire basket is a convenient size. To prepare for planting, stand it on a 10-in. pot or bucket so that it remains firm for handling.

Left—Place fibrous turfy loam in the bottom, up the sides and over the moss to a depth of 2–3 in. The loam and the moss will help to retain moisture.

HANGING BASKETS—FILLING

Below—Set trailing plants like lobelia in the side of the basket, easing the foliage carefully through the wires.

Above—Evenly space the plants around the basket and add more soil to cover the roots. Place more moss round the sides.

Below—When the moss and the fibrous turf are in place, firm round the outer edge so that it securely contains the compost.

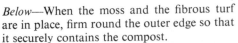

Above—Fill in the remaining space with soil, leaving a shallow depression in the centre. This is an aid to watering, an important cultural feature with hanging baskets.

HANGING BASKETS— PLANTING

Right—One of the most suitable plants for a hanging basket is ivy leaf geranium, which can be purchased in flower for an immediate effect.

Left—Set the plants fairly firmly. If two or three are planted at the outside for a trailing effect, set one in the centre for upright growth.

Right—Fuchsias, some of which are pendulous (weeping) varieties, and petunias are alternative choices. Always use a low-growing plant to fill in the base around the tall plants.

PLANTS IN POTS

Below—A simple but colourful display can be obtained by using a 10- or 12-in. pot. Polyanthus may be planted for spring flowering.

Above—The same pot may be planted with fuchsias, nasturtiums or ivy leaf geraniums for a summer display on a porch or verandah. Pay close attention to watering, especially if the pot stands in a warm place.

Below—Even a single geranium in a 7- or 8-in. pot will add some colour. Use well-grown plants and pot firmly. Do not stand out of doors until June.

Above—Large Dutch clogs make a novel and unusual feature. Stand flowering pot plants inside them.

PREPARATION OF SITE FOR A SHRUB

Left—A shrub border is a very suitable feature for a small garden and requires the minimum amount of attention. Even a dozen shrubs contribute a range of colour and interest over a long period.

Right—Dig the whole site where a new shrub border is to be planted to the full depth of the spade. Before the actual planting is done, draw a sketch plan on paper, showing where each subject is to be set.

Left—Even a single shrub like the diervilla in a bed or among stone work in a paved area will make an interesting feature. Small shrubs can be grown in wooden tubs or other containers.

PLANTING
A SHRUB—I

Right — Before planting, loosen the roots. It is important to handle these with care so none are broken.

Left—Plant climbers with the supporting cane in position. A mulch is beneficial, especially on light soils.

Right—Prune a clematis after planting. Cut back to a sound bud before fresh growth starts in the spring.

PLANTING A SHRUB—2

Left—On heavy soils, add peat and sand to the planting site. This aids quick establishment of newly planted climbers.

Right—Plants travel best in whalehide pots from the nursery. Soak pots in a bucket of water for a few minutes before planting. Ensure that soil-balls are saturated.

Left—Remove whalehide pots with care as well-grown plants have strong root systems.

ERECTING TRELLIS

Below—When fixing trellis to brickwork use thick rubber washers to keep the wood away from the wall.

Above—Drill three or four holes cleanly in the wood. Place the frame on the wall and mark where the holes will be sited.

Below—Drill the brickwork to take the screwing plugs. This enables the trellis to be removed for decorating.

Above—Push the screws through the holes in the woodwork and place on the rubber washers. Set in position on the wall and screw into place.

SUPPORTING CLIMBING SHRUBS ON TRELLIS

Left—Jasminum nudiflorum is an excellent shrub for flowering from December to February against a north-facing wall. Train against a wire mesh or wooden trellis.

Right—Clematis montana variety Pink Perfection does well on a cold wall or fence. Tie the main growths to supporting trellis or fence. A wide range of clematis is available from nurserymen.

*Left—*Train forsythia flat against a wall or a wooden slatted trellis. Forsythia does not climb, but like pyracantha and escallonia is often trained against a wall.

Right—Exposed newly planted shrubs may be protected from cold winds in winter by a temporary hessian screen. Remove this as soon as milder weather commences.

SHRUBS: CULTURAL POINTS—I

Left—Half standard flowering trees like prunus or malus need no pruning, except for shape. Do this in winter or after flowering.

Left—A weeping salix (willow) should have the main stem securely tied to a stake, to allow maximum weeping effect with the branches.

Right—In winter move heavy falls of snow off evergreen shrubs. Do this after every fall or the frozen snow will damage the shrubs.

SHRUBS: CULTURAL POINTS—2

Left—Cut off the dead heads and faded flowers of lilac. No other pruning is necessary.

Right—Early summer flowering shrubs like weigela (shown here), philadelphus and forsythia need some of the older wood cut out after flowering. Leave the young shoots which will bear flowers the following year.

Left—Shrubs like buddleia flower on shoots made the same season. When pruning cut the annual growth well back in late March.

Right—Dead flower heads being removed from dwarf lavender (*Lavendula nana compacta*). If flower heads are to be cut and kept, take them off when they are nearly fully open.

SHRUBS—PLANTING FROM POTS

Left—Smash the pot to release the roots of an established shrub which have extended through the drainage hole. If only a few roots extend through the drainage hole they can be severed.

Right—Rhododendrons being planted. Bear in mind that they need acid soil—soil not containing lime. Add peat or leafmould to the planting site.

Left—Remove the plant carefully from its container. Do not disturb the root ball, and set the plant in position a little deeper than before.

Right—Carefully firm round the outside of the soil ball. Mulch with a 3- or 4-in. layer of peat or leafmould and water regularly in dry spells.

SHRUBS—PLANTING FROM CONTAINERS

Below—With the increase of garden centres shrubs can be purchased in cans, pots and other containers. When planting shrubs from 10-in. whale-hide pots take out a hole large enough to take the ball of soil comfortably.

Above—Break the whale-hide pot by splitting at the seam. Keep the ball of soil intact, thus ensuring no check after planting. This is especially important with conifers.

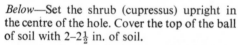

Below—Set the shrub (cupressus) upright in the centre of the hole. Cover the top of the ball of soil with 2–2½ in. of soil.

Above—Firm the soil after planting and mulch with peat or compost as an aid to moisture retention. Plant shrubs from pots or containers at any time of the year.

GARDEN POOL—CONSTRUCTION

Left—The foundation of a concrete pool is the most important factor. Ensure that the base is made very strong with brick bats, iron bars and anything which will bind the cement.

Right—Fit shelves, before the final rendering is applied, to cater for water plants which require shallow water.

Left—Edge the pool with stone slabs or crazy paving. Place the slabs to protrude over the edge of the pond. Trowel on the final coat of cement about $\frac{1}{2}$ in. thick.

GARDEN POOL—CONSTRUCTION

Left—An effective combination of waterfall and pool can be easily constructed from pre-formed fibreglass or plastic units. *Below left*—Alternatively, a plastic liner provides another simple method of pool making.

Above right—Water for cascades and waterfalls can be recirculated by means of a pump. The simplest type, the submersible pump, is placed in position. *Right*—A small pump installed outside the pool from which the water is drawn and recirculated by means of pipes.

GARDEN POOL— PLANT CONTAINERS

Left—Wire baskets make ideal plant and compost containers for water lilies. *Below left*—Split bamboo baskets, obtainable from greengrocers, make large plant containers.

Above right—Rot-proof plastic containers, in which a number of holes have been bored, are long-lasting and modern. *Right*—Plant aerating pond plants in shallow pans of sandy compost. They are vital to keep the pool fresh and clean.

GARDEN POOL PLANTING—I

Right—Firm the soil with a wooden rammer. Do this when the basket is half-full, packing the soil well into the bottom and around the joints of the partly rotted turves which have been used to line the basket. A sprinkling of bonemeal is placed between the turves and the compost, which should be of a medium heavy texture and contain some rotted cow manure.

Left—Set the root into the centre. When the basket is half-full the crown of the lily should be level with the rim. Put more soil around the roots and again ram in place.

Right—Soak the soil until it is thoroughly wetted. This prevents too much soil being subsequently washed away. Lower gently into the pool, taking care not to disturb the soil or plant.

GARDEN POOL—ROUTINE WORK

Below—Waterside plants should be planted in pockets built into the side of the pool. Leave sufficient space for the water to come into contact with the soil and roots.

Above—Top-dress waterside containers each spring with pieces of rotted turf loam. Work the pieces around the plants.

Below—Make a regular habit of removing any rubbish which falls into the pool.

Above—Take off all the spent flower heads. This important job applies to both lilies and rushes.

Right—Pull up old water lily leaves, with as much stem as possible, when they begin to go rotten.

GARDEN POOL—AUTUMN WORK

Left—Cut the old growth away as the plants die back at the end of the season. If left they become a refuge for pests.

Left—Collect small leaves and pieces of rubbish from the water with a piece of fine mesh fitted over the tines of a garden fork.

Right—Make a hole carefully through ice to enable the fish to breathe. A hole will not be necessary if there are only plants in the pool.

CONSTRUCTING A ROCK GARDEN—I

Left—Rock gardens vary in construction. Some have bold stone faces, as here, or the rock can be partly buried to give the impression of strata.

Right—"Rock banks" are a popular choice in small gardens. Plant them with a wide range of low growing plants to give colour over a long period.

Left—Soil which has been excavated for a garden pool may be used in the construction of a rockery. Rock or stone can be used as available or purchased.

CONSTRUCTING A ROCK GARDEN—2

Left—Build small rockeries on a level surface which is slightly raised. This gives an improved appearance to the plants when in flower and to the stones.

Right—Position the stones and push soil firmly round and under each one. Light and sandy well-drained soil is best for rock plants.

Left—Make up soil pockets as shown, keeping the line of stone work so that it resembles strata or outcrops.

Right—Vary the soil in individual pockets to suit the special needs of plants—lime-hating plants require pockets of peat and sand.

GROWING PLANTS FOR A ROCK GARDEN

Left—Grow young plants in 3-in. pots until the rock garden is ready for them.

Right—Pot the plants firmly in a potting compost of two parts loam, two parts sand and one part peat. Crock the pots well to ensure sharp, quick drainage.

Left—Directly after potting, surface the compost with a $\frac{1}{4}$-in. layer of gravel chippings. Do not use limestone chippings as many plants dislike lime.

CULTURAL AIDS
IN A ROCK GARDEN

Below—Set the plants in small pockets between stones so that each has an individual site and can be seen to advantage.

Above—Give ericas a mulch of peat by applying a 1–2-in. layer in the spring. Most ericas do best in soil containing no lime.

Below—Place gravel chippings around the crowns of plants such as saxifrage. This ensures sharp drainage and adds an attractive appearance.

Above—Eradicate broad-leafed and deep-rooted weeds which grow between the stones by using a "Touchweeder" stick.

ROCK PLANTS

Right—Cut back aubrieta which has finished flowering and is untidy and straggly with withered leaves and stems, to leave 3 or 4 in. of the old growth.

Left—Plants will benefit from being cut back, although the clump will have a dry and dead appearance for a time.

Right—The plants quickly begin to grow again, becoming an attractive mound of young, green leaves.

TROUGH GARDEN—1

Left—Stone troughs with a pleasingly weathered and matured appearance are ideal to use.

Right—Cover the drainage hole of the trough with fairly large pieces of crock.

Left—Modern pre-cast sinks invariably have a number of drainage holes. Cover the whole of the base.

Right—Place 1 in. of fibrous turfy loam over the crocks. Then fill with an open mixture of compost to ensure good drainage.

TROUGH GARDEN—2

Left—Firm the compost evenly all over, paying special attention at the ends and sides.

Right—Plant a dwarf conifer to add height and pieces of small stones for added interest. Granite chippings around the plants give colour to the trough.

Left—Position the plants with consideration to their method of growth and eventual size. Trailing plants should be kept to the edge.

Right—Pay careful attention to watering and the removal of dead flowers, which considerably improves the appearance of the trough.

MAINTENANCE OF A HEDGE—I

Left—A hedge has a number of uses in the garden. It can act as a wind break or an evergreen barrier between a flower and a vegetable garden.

Right—Clip the hedge regularly about four times a year, otherwise the base becomes bare and empty and the top straggly.

Left—Cut back the old growth of a neglected hedge to about 18 in. to 2 ft in early spring. Young shoots will develop from the base.

MAINTENANCE OF A HEDGE—2

Left—Remove long grass and weeds from the base of the hedge each spring. Cut with a grass hook but take care not to damage the hedge.

Right—Hoe off the remaining weeds and grass roots, using a draw hoe and rake.

Left—Spray the base of the hedge and the grass at the base with a proprietary insecticide to prevent pests being harboured.

Right—Apply a general fertiliser at 4 oz. to the sq. yd in spring. This ensures sturdy growth and good colour in the leaves.

TRIMMING A HEDGE WITH SHEARS

Left — Cut the sides of the hedge first, holding the shears flat to the hedge-face.

Right—Secure a line, with the aid of poles, at the height at which the top of the hedge is to be cut, supporting the line in the centre if it sags.

Left—Cut first along the whole length of the line with the shears turned over. This will give a guide when the line is removed.

Right—Stand on a stool and cut along the top of the hedge. You should be able to look down on the hedge as you cut it.

Right—Place the electric cable over the left shoulder, keeping it safely away from the blades.

TRIMMING A HEDGE WITH ELECTRIC CLIPPERS

Left—Oil electric hedge clippers regularly when they are in use. Sap from the hedge clippings removes the oil and impairs the efficiency of the blades.

Left—Tilt the cutting blade slightly inwards towards the hedge. Do not place the blade flat against the hedge.

Right—Work from left to right towards the uncut part of the hedge, cutting upwards with smooth sweeps.

EQUIPMENT—1

Right—This lightweight set of tools, comprising a border spade, border fork, grubber, trowel and hand fork, is obtainable as a set for ladies.

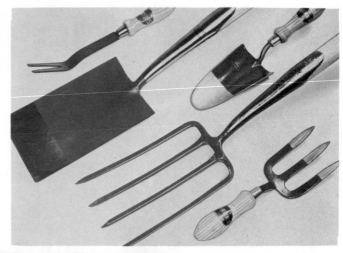

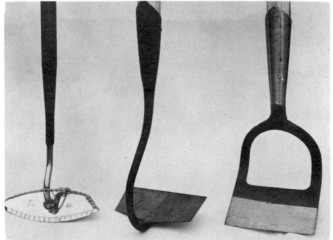

Left—A hoe is an essential piece of equipment. Several types are shown here—Dutch hoe on the right and draw hoe second from the right.

Right—After use, tools should be cleaned and lightly oiled and stored in a clean, dry place. A tool rack ensures that everything is to hand when needed.

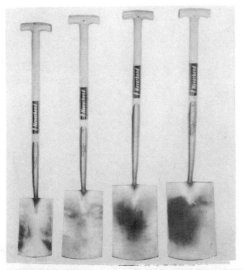

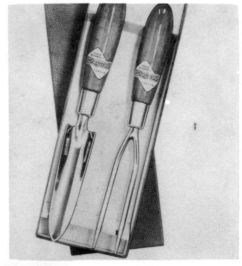

EQUIPMENT—2

Above left—A spade is an essential piece of gardening equipment. A lightweight ladies' spade is shown on the left, but a slightly heavier model is needed for general digging.

Above right—Trowel and hand forks, specially designed for weeding and planting in the rock garden, are extremely useful.

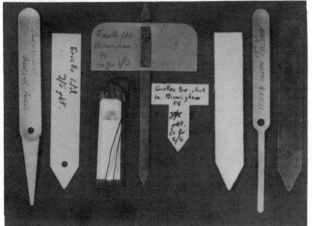

Above—Use only strong and durable labels for labelling plants. Many types are available.

Right—Dual-purpose tools, with a number of different combinations, are available for many jobs.

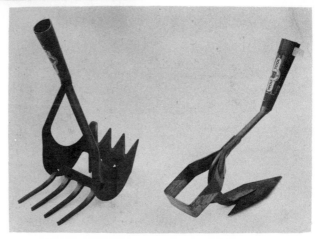

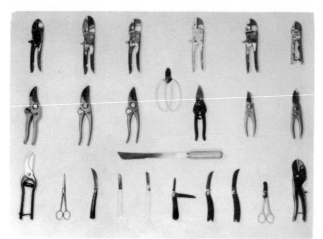

EQUIPMENT—3

Left—Sécateurs are available to suit individual requirements and various jobs.

Below—Conversion kits for power drills enable hedges to be cut easily. Be very careful not to cut the cable or you may receive a 240-volt shock.

Below left—A sharp knife is an essential piece of equipment for taking cuttings. Keep it for garden use only and it will retain a sharp edge longer.

Below right—An ideal saw, with backward-pointing teeth and a curved blade, for general garden work and lopping branches in awkward positions.

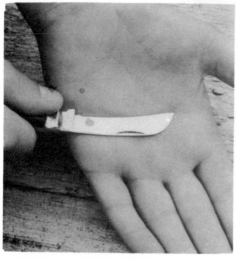

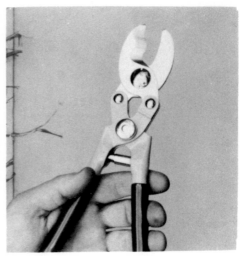

EQUIPMENT—4

Above left—Use long-handled pruners for pruning tall or half standard trees, both flowering and fruiting varieties. This is safer than a ladder when working in awkward places.

Above right—Cut extra thick wood with double-action, parrot-billed pruning sécateurs.

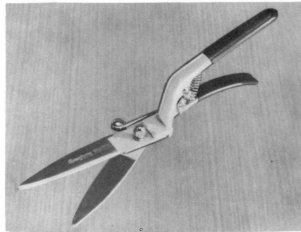

Above—This light and efficient tool can be held in one hand when trimming hedges and lawns.

Right—Use only good shears for clipping hedges. Many types are available, designed for both men and women.

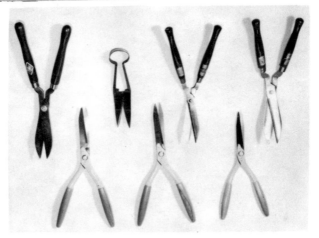

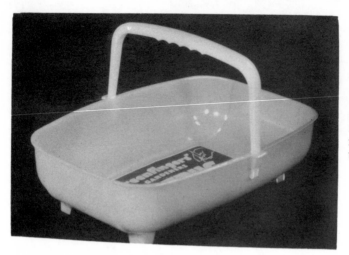

EQUIPMENT—5

Left—Use a "Trug" or a garden basket for weeding or gathering fruit and vegetables. Modern types are made from plastic which resists corrosion and rotting.

Right—Small hand barrows make gardening operations easier. The long handle makes wheeling possible without bending down.

Left — A small portable, pressure-fed flame-gun can be used for destroying weeds on garden paths or between crazy paving. It can also be used for sterilising seed beds.

EQUIPMENT—6

Right—Hose connections and fittings for taps are available in varying shapes and sizes.

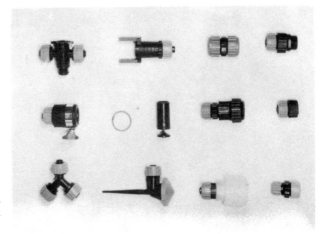

Below—Keep a garden hose on a reel to prevent kinking and to ensure a longer life.

Above—Apply weedkillers to a lawn with a spray-bar, ensuring even distribution of the liquid.

Left—A selection of syringes, with hose attachments for use with buckets.

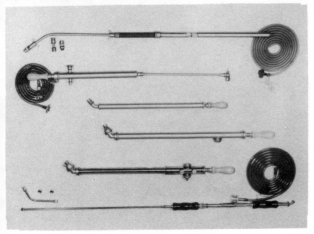

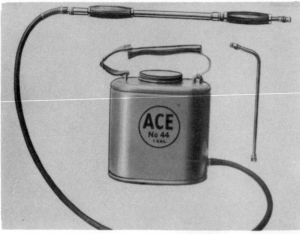

EQUIPMENT—7

Left—Use a knapsack sprayer for large areas. It is easily carried by the handle or readily converted into a shoulder strap.

Below left—Hand-pressure sprayers of moulded polythene are light and easy to use and very quickly cleaned.

Above right—Spot-treat small infestations of pests or diseases with a small sprayer. It is easy to fill and the spray should be applied at a good pressure.

Right—Apply dusting powders with a dust gun. The bellows, rotary and hand-puffer sprayers shown here are available to suit different requirements.

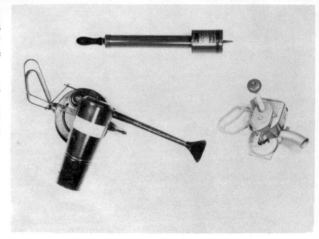

PESTS AND DISEASES—1

Left—Slugs attack both young plants and seedlings, especially during mild, damp weather or mild weather following rain. Control a slug infestation by applying baits of slug pellets around plants which are affected.

Right—Caterpillar damage on roses affects the foliage and flower buds. Apply derris or pyrethrum as soon as the damage is noticed. Use dusts only when the foliage is damp.

Left—Red spiders seriously affect violets and polyanthus plants, especially in warm, dry summers. Reduce the attacks by growing the plants in semi-shade and where they will receive plenty of moisture.

PESTS AND DISEASES—2

Right—Leaf miners severely damage chrysanthemum leaves. The larvae feed within the leaf tissue, causing channels, as shown. Spray with nicotine, BHC or malathion at the first sign of attack.

Left—Leaf cutter bees cut pieces from the edges of the leaves. The damage is not serious and flowers and shoots are not affected.

Right—Greenfly seriously attack cinerarias. The aphides secrete a sticky residue all over the leaves. Control this with nicotine sprays.

PESTS AND DISEASES—3

Left—Rust, diseases attack antirrhinums, although certain varieties are resistant to this disease. Symptoms of attack are shown here.

Right—Some varieties of rose are very susceptible to attacks of mildew, but roses with thick, green, glossy foliage are more resistant. Control mildew with a Karathane preparation.

Left—Gladioli are attacked by a disease causing a yellowing of the foliage. Dust all the corms with one of the proprietary fungicides before storing during the winter.

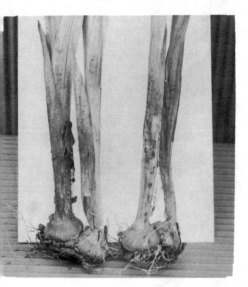

Right—Fasciation of a delphinium stem. The cause is not clearly understood, but it is thought to be due to a breakdown in the make-up of the cells. It is not a disease, but a distortion of the stems.

PESTS AND DISEASES—4

Left—Mildew on delphiniums severely checks growth. At the first sign of attack, dust with a sulphur powder. Keep the soil well watered.

Right—Fungi and toadstool growths often appear in large numbers on a lawn. "Switch" them off with a birch besom broom and dust the growths with lawn sand to eradicate them.

Left—Weather conditions cause damage in many ways. Warm damp weather causes "balling" of rose buds.

PROPAGATION

Right—Bottomless black paper tubes can be used for many vegetable and flower seeds. When the tray is full, pour soil over the pots until they are full and firm; then plant seed or seedlings. At a later date, each plant comes out of the box without root disturbance.

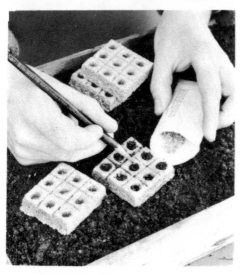

Right—The Jiffy Pot range is now quite wide and as many as sixty of these peat pots can now be fitted into a standard seed tray. They are easy to handle and require very little compost to fill, transplanting is easy and plants suffer no check.

SOWING CONTAINERS

Left—Sweet pea seeds being sown in Multi-pots. These plastic containers are light and easy to handle, and save space. Young plants grow on in these and pricking out is unnecessary.

Left—Vermiculite squares are best placed in boxes of damp peat whilst the seed is germinating. Place a little soil in each depression before sowing. The moisture-holding properties of vermiculite are a great asset in this method of sowing.

SOIL BLOCKS

Left—A small soil block mould (obtainable from a garden sundriesman) being used to make blocks 3 in. by 3 in. The compost needs to be slightly damper than it is normally used to ensure that the blocks retain their shape when being made. The mould is filled firmly with compost, and the base fixed to a piece of wood.

Right—A sowing or planting depression is made with the plate on the right in the soil block before it is placed over the base. Then the block is pressed firmly down while the side grips are held; it will then stand free and can be moved to a tray.

Left—As the blocks are made, stand them in a tray with a ½-in. layer of peat placed in the bottom. Sowing or pricking out of seedlings can then proceed. As the plant or seed grows, the roots hold the block together. Watering is best done into the peat, from which the blocks will absorb moisture.

SAVING FLOWER SEEDS

Left—Where flower seeds are allowed to ripen on the plant, gather the "heads" when quite dry and store in an airy place. The seed heads can then be put temporarily in a polythene bag, which also prevents seed being lost. *Below*—If the seed is to be sown immediately after gathering, shake the heads over a prepared container. With many flower seeds, it is sound practice to sow as the seed becomes ripe.

Above—Seeds may also be shaken out onto a piece of white paper and then tipped into a small packet for ease of sowing. If they are not for immediate use, store the seeds in a dry place until required and label the container. *Right*—Seeds may also be sown from the hand: take the seed between thumb and finger and space evenly over the surface of the pot.

PREPARING A SEED TRAY

Right—A wide space at the base of a seed tray must be covered with crocks. This need not be done where the space is only ¼ in. wide or less.

Below—

To economise with sowing compost and to retain moisture, cover the crocks and bottom of the tray with a ½-in. layer of damp peat.

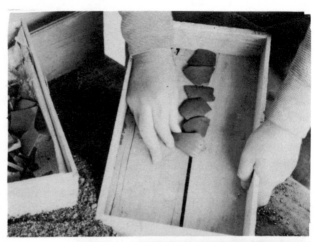

Above—After filling the seed tray, firm the compost with the fingers. Make sure that the corners and sides of the tray are given the same attention as the centre, and that the compost is firmed evenly. *Left*—When the seed tray is filled, level off the top, using a pressing board or a piece of wood about 12 in. by 3 in.

SOWING IN A TRAY—I

Right—Prepare the surface of the compost by sieving some fine soil over the made-up seed tray.

Below—Cut a piece of cane a little shorter than the width of the tray.

Above—Press the cane into the soil at intervals to make shallow drills about $\frac{1}{8}$ in. deep. The number of drills is governed by the amount of seed to be sown. *Left*—Sow the seed from the packet, resting the hand on a piece of wood laid flat across the tray to act as a support. This avoids over-thick and uneven sowing.

SOWING
IN A TRAY—2

Right—Where several different kinds or varieties are being sown in the same tray, label each row separately as soon as it is sown. This ensures that names are not mixed.

Left—Water carefully with a fine rosed can so that the seeds are not disturbed — especially important with small seeds. An alternative method of watering is to place the bottom of the box in water until the surface becomes damp.

Right—Even germination is ensured by enclosing the tray in a polythene bag slightly larger than the tray. This covering keeps the temperature a few degrees higher and gives quicker germination.

SOWING IN A POT—I

Left—For sowing small batches of seed, use a 3½- or 5-in. pot, a half-pot being a suitable container. Cover the drainage holes with pieces of crock. Pots must be clean, and if not new, washed beforehand.

Right—Cover the crocks with about 1 in. of turf fibre, which should first be teased apart. Alternatively peat may be used. Press this down fairly firmly, then fill the pot with J.I. seed compost.

Left—After filling the pot with compost and firming evenly level the surface, using the base of a small pot. Leave ½ in. between the top of the pot and the compost as watering space.

SOWING IN A POT—2

Right—Small seeds, which are not easy to see, should first be tipped out on a sheet of white paper with the size of the pot to be used for sowing marked out. This amount of seed is then poured into a small container for the actual sowing. *Below*—With small quantities of seed, two kinds can be sown in the same pot, with a label placed across the centre to act as a division. Label each kind of seed clearly with its name and date of sowing.

Above—Cover the seed with finely sieved soil. Large seeds should be covered by about $\frac{1}{4}$ in., smaller seeds more shallowly. Very small seeds should not be covered, but simply pressed into the surface. *Left*—After sowing, water the pots carefully with a fine rosed watering can or stand them in a bowl of water so that the moisture soaks upward through the drainage hole. Avoid over-saturation, particularly with small pots; it is best to watch the surface and remove the pot as soon as it appears damp.

CACTI FROM SEED

Above left—When small quantities of different cactus are being sown, divide the pot into three or four sections, with pieces of celluloid labels pushed into the compost. Number the sections for identification. *Above right*—Tip the seed into a tablespoon and gently shake the seed from this, spreading it as evenly as possible. Cactus seed germinates best if left on the surface.

Above—After watering the pots, which is best done by standing them in water, drain and place them in a propagating frame and cover with a piece of glass and a sheet of black paper. *Left*—When pricking out seedlings, which resemble tiny beads, use an old plastic knitting needle with a cleft cut into it. Handle with care, as broken roots will cause the seedling to die.

DELPHINIUMS FROM SEED

Below—A small batch of seed may be sown in a pot or seed tray in August in J.I. seed compost or in April under glass. Lift the seedlings when large enough to handle, taking care to keep the root system intact.

Above—Prick out six seedlings to a seed tray in some J.I.P.I. Delphiniums make a large fibrous root system, and by pricking out only six to a tray overcrowding is avoided and plants do not need to be moved again until planting out. Trays may be stood outdoors.

Below—Young plants can also be pricked out into 3½-in. pots when a few especially good batches of plants are needed or when planting out may be delayed.

Above—Seedlings which have been grown on in boxes and have become strong plants can be planted into a nursery bed to overwinter. The soil should be rich and fibrous. Set plants out at 9 in. apart; the roots being very fine, care should be taken when firming.

Right—Chipping the skin of sweet pea seed. This is a good practice with hard-skinned seeds, helping towards even and speedy growth. Use a small penknife to lift a tiny portion of the skin.

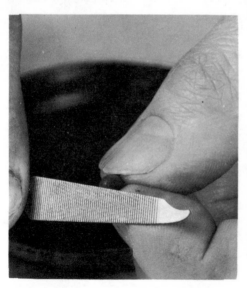

Right—Special pots may be bought for sweet peas, deeper than normal so that the long roots which are made have plenty of space in which to develop. Sow with a dibber, five or six seeds to a pot.

SWEET PEAS FROM SEED

Left—Before sowing prepare a seed label for each variety. Seed bought by name is packed with the variety stamped on the packet, and a seed label should be prepared for each before the packet is opened. Use a waterproof pencil.

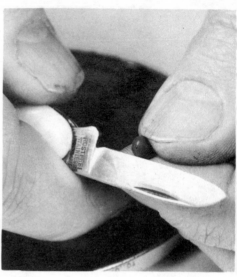

Left—A nail file may also be used to smooth away the skin of a hard-skinned seed until the kernel is exposed. Whether a knife or a nail file is used, the seed should be treated on the opposite side to the eye.

AIDS TO SOWING

Left—A simple aid to germination in the absence of a greenhouse is to enclose the pot in a polythene bag after sowing, sealing the end of the bag with an elastic band. This creates a slightly warmer atmosphere. The pot or pan will not require watering again until the seeds have germinated, when the seedlings must be removed from the bag.

Right—A wooden box may be used as a small propagating frame: place a 4–6-in. layer of damp peat over the bottom so that pots can be plunged to their rims in the peat to conserve moisture. Place sheets of glass over the box, not forgetting to leave a small gap for air.

Left—A wide range of seeds can be obtained ready sown in containers from garden sundries shops. These need only to be watered through holes punched in the top of the container, as directed, and stood in a temperature of 50° F. They need not be kept in a greenhouse; a well-lit window sill will give the conditions required for germination.

RAISING SEEDLINGS

Left—Where a variety of seeds is being grown, $3\frac{1}{2}$-in. pots are suitable containers. When germination is apparent the pots should be stood where they will benefit from the maximum amount of daylight.

Right—Stand peat or similar pots in a seed tray or shallow box for ease of handling. Place 1 in. of peat at the bottom of the box. This will help to keep the pots moist.

Left—Cyclamen of different varieties being grown in the same tray. In such a case divide the tray and label each division clearly. At a later stage, move these young plants on into $3\frac{1}{2}$-in. pots.

PRICKING OUT

Right—Seedlings being pricked out into 2-in. paper tubes. Use J.I.P. 1 compost for this purpose. Handle the seedlings by the leaves and set them so that the lower leaves are just above the surface of the compost. *Below*— A peat block with cavities filled with J.I.P. 1. The seedlings are pricked out in these and the block stood in a seed tray. On planting out, the block is divided into single plants.

Above—Seedlings being pricked out into a seed tray. Here two different subjects are being grown on in one tray. Flower seedlings can be pricked out 54 to a seed tray, i.e. in rows 9 by 6, but for small batches 40 to each tray is adequate. *Left*—A good example of spaced sowing of gloxinias. The seeds are spaced out at sowing time and pricking out may not be necessary, particularly if the young plants are to be grown in pots subsequently.

Right—A wooden rake is a useful tool for breaking down the surface soil in preparation for seed sowing. Biennials or perennials sown in May or June and seed rows for cut flower purposes all require the same preparation.

Right—If the soil is heavy, add a half-and-half mixture of peat and sand at the rate of 1 lb. per sq. yd. Rake into the top few inches of soil.

PREPARING A SEEDBED

Left—After the seedbed has been dug o: forked through, break down the surface soi with the tines of a fork to obtain the neces sary tilth (fine soil) in which to sow the seeds Prepare especially well for small flower seeds

Left—A dressing of superphosphate may be applied before sowing at 3 oz. per sq. yd to ensure good root action for seedlings and young plants. Rake in the fertiliser evenly with an iron rake.

DRILLS AND THEIR PROTECTION

Below—Another method of drawing drills is to use the handle of an iron rake, pressing this into finely prepared soil to a depth of $\frac{1}{2}$ in.

Above—After sowing, cover the drills with a sprinkling of grass mowings as a protection against birds. Seed rows are easily damaged by birds "dusting" in dry soil.

Below—Drills can also be made with the back of the rake head. Even depth of drill is important, otherwise germination will be erratic.

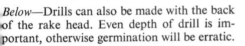

Above—If the soil is very dry, draw the drills 2 in. deep and fill in 1 in. at the base with moist peat, or water the drill before sowing.

SOWING FLOWER SEEDS

Left—Seed of many perennials like lupins, delphiniums and scabious may be sown outdoors in May and June. Drills should be ½ in. deep and 6 in. apart.

Right—Sow thinly so that the seeds are spaced about ½ in. apart. This will prevent overcrowding and ensure better development of the young plants.

Left—Cover the seeds by drawing the soil into the drills to an even depth with an iron rake. Firm the soil evenly with the head of the rake.

Right—Label each row at the time of sowing. A small seedbed with short rows will be adequate for average home gardening purposes.

CHRYSANTHEMUM CUTTINGS—I

Right—Take cuttings when growth on the old stools is well developed; shoots 3 in. long and of diary pencil thickness are suitable. Do not use thick or overgrown cuttings. *Below*— To prepare cuttings, remove the leaves by pulling them away from the stem. The growing points are extremely tender and brittle, and care in handling is essential.

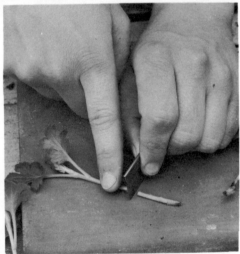

Above—Next prepare the base by cutting through the shoot to leave it 2–2½ in. long. Cut cleanly just below a leaf joint with a single-edged razor blade. *Left*—Dip the base of the cutting into a hormone rooting aid. This is especially useful if only a few cuttings are being taken and 100-per-cent rooting is required.

CHRYSANTHEMUM CUTTINGS—2

Right—For rooting small batches, 3½-in. pots are best. Cover the compost in the pots with a layer of sharp sand; a little of this trickles into the holes and aids rooting. *Below*—If aphides are present, dip the prepared cuttings before insertion in a nicotine solution. This will also destroy any leaf miner which may be present.

Above — Cuttings root more readily when inserted round the edge of the pot. Six is an ideal number for the size shown here. Each cutting must be made firm. *Left*—When space is limited, strike cuttings in seed trays, keeping varieties in rows. Label the rows for identification.

DAHLIA CUTTINGS—I

Right—Take shoots from tubers started into growth in a heated greenhouse in February. Do not use any that are thick or hollow. *Below*—Prepare the cuttings by removing the lower leaves. Shoots may be taken with a small piece of parent tuber still attached; in this case it is not necessary to trim below a joint.

Above—Use a razor blade of the type shown here to prepare the cuttings where a piece of tuber is not attached. Cut clearly just below a leaf joint, using a firm surface. *Left*—Dip the base of each cutting first in water and then in a hormone rooting aid. Tap to remove surplus powder.

DAHLIA CUTTINGS—2

Below—5-in. pots are best for small batches of cuttings. Spread a thin layer of sharp sand over the surface and make firm and level.

Below—After 2–3 weeks, spread the fingers through the cuttings, turn the pot over and carefully knock the plants out. Roots will be showing and the cuttings ready for potting on singly in 3½-in pots. Use J.I.P. 1 compost.

Above—When inserting the cuttings, ensure that the base is touching the soil at the bottom. Firm the compost around each one firmly as it is put in. Take care not to overwater; the cuttings may rot if kept too damp.

Above—When potting handle the plants with care, as the roots are brittle. Do not plant out of doors until danger of frost has passed.

Right—Strip off the lower skin from the base of the shoot with the fingers. No leaves should be removed from young cuttings.

DELPHINIUM CUTTINGS

Left—Take young shoots for use as cuttings when 3–4 in. long in spring. To obtain earlier cuttings, lift a few crowns and plant in a cold frame in winter.

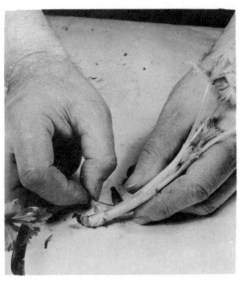

Left—Cut through the base of the shoot cleanly with either a sharp knife or a razor blade.

Right—Insert the cuttings in a sandy compost in pots, setting them firmly. Do not overwater. Keep the pots in a cold frame or cold greenhouse until the cuttings are well rooted, then plant outdoors.

FUCHSIA CUTTINGS

Left — Take young shoots, produced by plants stored in the greenhouse, early in spring as 2–3 in. cuttings. Remove the two lower leaves and cut through below the leaf joint with a razor blade.

Right—Plant the cuttings fairly close together in 5-in. pots. A suitable rooting medium, in which the cuttings can also grow on for a while, is three parts loam, two parts sharp sand and one part peat (by bulk).

Left—Cover each pot with a polythene bag. This gives quicker rooting and helps to stop wilting. Leave 4 in. between the top of the cuttings and the bag. A rubber band round the bottom of the pot holds the polythene in place.

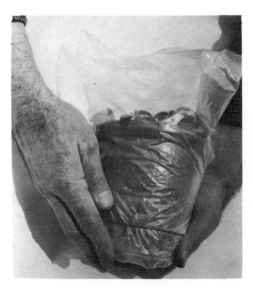

Right—Strong-rooted plants will develop quickly with a little care. If plants are intended to be grown on for greenhouse or house decoration, pot them on into 5-in. pots. For bedding work, $3\frac{1}{2}$-in. pots will do.

GERANIUM CUTTINGS

Left—A cutting prepared for insertion, basal cut made just below a leaf joint and lower leaves removed cleanly. A rooting hormone powder applied to the base speeds rooting.

Right—Cuttings being inserted round the edge of a 5-in. pot. A sharp sandy compost is best: 3 parts sharp sand, 1 part each peat and loam. Ensure that the base of each cutting is touching the bottom. Make very firm.

Left—Deep seed boxes may be used instead of pots where space is limited. Make up the boxes with the same compost as for pots and plant the cuttings 3 in. apart. Water on the soil, not the leaves, to prevent damping off.

Right—When cuttings have been taken in the autumn and become strong-rooted plants, the tips can be cut off in spring and used as further cuttings.

GERANIUM LEAF
BUD CUTTINGS

Below—1-in. long pieces containing a leaf joint, with a leaf bud showing, are economical. Cut ½ in. above and below the joint.

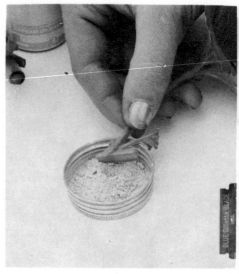

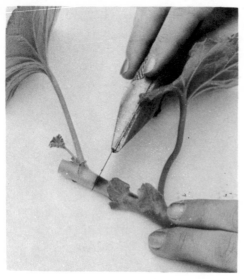

Above—Cut the 1-in. stub in half, discard the half without the bud and dip the half with the bud into the hormone powder, ensuring that the surface is well covered.

Below—Pot each cutting separately, making sure that only the top is left above the soil. Firm evenly all round with a dibber. A peat pot which can be kept damp without direct watering is best.

Above—A young rooted bud cutting ready for potting on. These cuttings make roots fairly quickly and soon fill the small peat pots.

HYDRANGEA CUTTINGS

Left—Take a shoot from low down on the side of the parent plant in spring when the plants are being grown in the greenhouse.

Right—Cut through the base of the shoot between two buds (i.e. at an "internodal point") leaving the tip intact. Cut off the lower leaves cleanly.

Left—Insert the cuttings firmly in vermiculite or a sandy compost such as three parts sharp sand and one part each peat and loam. Water with care and not too much.

Right—Rooted cutting ready for potting on ingly into a 3-in. pot. If blue flowers are equired, do not use a potting compost containing lime at any stage.

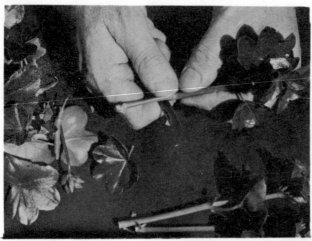

IVY LEAF GERANIUM CUTTINGS

Left—Suitable cuttings can usually be found at the ends of the main and side shoots. Take cuttings about 6 in. long cleanly with a sharp knife. Prepare them by removing the lower leaves and cutting through just below the joint. *Below*—Trimmed cuttings ready for insertion: they are now about 4 in. long. Leave for 12 hours to wilt before inserting.

Below left—Prepare a 5-in. pot with a sand, peat and compost mixture (in equal proportions) surfaced with $\frac{1}{4}$ in. of silver sand, so that a little of the sand will go into the hole as the cutting is inserted. *Below right*—The medium used for striking cuttings does not contain sufficient nutriment for the plants to grow on once they are rooted. Cuttings should therefore be potted on as soon as possible after a good root formation has been made.

LUPIN CUTTINGS

Left — Where further plants are required from a selected plant, such as one with a particularly fine colour, young shoots may be taken in spring when 4–5 in. long for use as cuttings.

Right—Shoots as taken from the parent plant. Avoid using very thick or thin and weak shoots.

Left—Prepare the shoots by trimming off the lower leaves and cutting cleanly through the base with a sharp knife or razor blade.

Right—Insert cuttings into a 5-in. pot or half pot, using a compost of 3 parts loam, 2 parts sharp sand and 1 part peat with a thin layer of sand on top. Keep in a cold frame or a cold greenhouse until cuttings are well rooted.

CUTTINGS FROM PINKS AND BORDER CARNATIONS

Left—Suitable cuttings can be found around the outsides of the old clumps, and are best taken in June or July. Remove lower leaves by pulling them off. *Below*—Trim the cuttings with a sharp knife just below a joint. Each should have two or three leaves left apart from the growing point, and be about 3 to 4 in. long when prepared.

Below left—Although pinks and carnations strike quite easily, a dipping in rooting powder guarantees quicker rooting. It will be found simplest to bunch a number together when doing this. *Below right*—Cover the compost in the pot with silver sand and insert the cuttings over the surface to about a third of their length and an inch apart, ensuring that each is quite firm. Give a good watering.

MULTIPLE ROOTING

Left—This is a method of rooting a number of cuttings of many soft wood kinds. Take a 12-by-6-in. strip of polythene and lay a $\frac{1}{4}$-in. layer of damp moss along half the width. *Below*—Prepare cuttings by the normal method. Dip them in hormone powder and lay them side by side on the moss $\frac{1}{2}$–1 in. apart.

Below—Fold over the other half of the polythene to cover the base of the cuttings and proceed to roll, keeping the moss on the outside. Keep the roll firm and secure with a rubber band. Stand in a warm, light position. As soon as roots develop, plant into a seed box containing sandy loam.

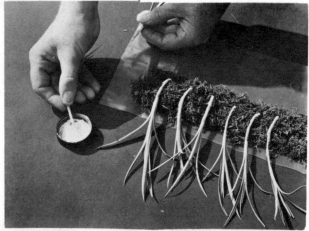

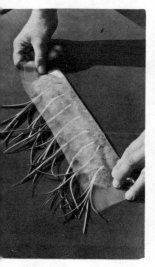

SOFT WOOD CUTTINGS

Left—Use young, short, soft side shoots 3– in. long taken in May. Prepare by removing leaves from lower half of cutting.

Right—Cut through at the base just below a leaf joint, using a sharp knife or razor blade.

Left—Dip bases of prepared cuttings in a hormone rooting aid before insertion. This treatment gives quicker and better rooting.

Right—Insert cuttings in a cold frame in a sandy compost at 3-in. spacing. The frame should be kept "close", i.e. very little ventilation should be given, until the cuttings are rooted.

HARD WOOD CUTTINGS

Below—Cuttings can be taken in October from such shrubs as philadelphus, buddleia, forsythia, ribes and many others. All root fairly easily from young shoots made during the current season.

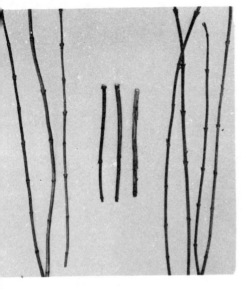

Above—Prepare cuttings of privet 9–10 in. long. Discard the thin end and cut just below a bud at the base. The same preparation is suitable for the other hard wood shrubs.

Below—Prepare a V trench with a spade, leaving a slightly sloping back for the cuttings to rest on. Push the bottoms of the cuttings firmly into the soil at 6-in. spacing.

Above—Firm cuttings with the foot after insertion. It may be necessary to repeat this after a severe frost, as they may become loosened when frozen soil thaws out.

Right—A length of the parent stem will be attached to the heel shoot: pare this with a sharp knife.

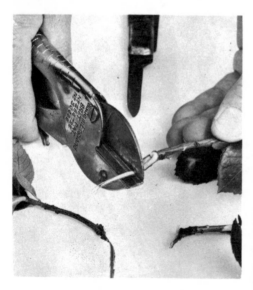

Right—Finally, remove the lower leaves to half the length of the cutting with a sharp knife.

HEEL CUTTINGS

Left—Pull off a side-shoot 3–4 in. long with a "heel". Hold the shoot close to the stem with finger and thumb and pull downwards towards the base. June or July is the time for taking half-ripe cuttings.

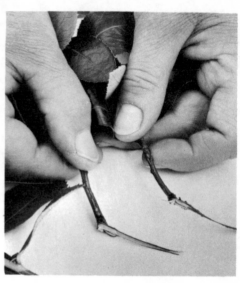

Left—Trim the long tail on the heel, leaving about $\frac{1}{2}$ in. of old wood. Cut cleanly through with sécateurs. Trim rough edges cleanly with a knife.

LAVENDER CUTTINGS

Right—Take off side-growths from the base of the plant in June. It is always best to replace lavender bushes before they become straggly.

Below—
Many semi-ripe wood cuttings root better if a small heel is left.

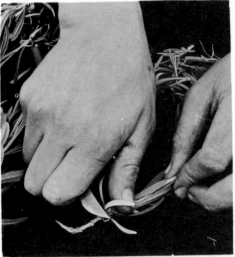

Above—Dip the cuttings with lower leaves removed in a hormone rooting powder before insertion. *Left*—Insert the cuttings in a seed tray, in a compost of three parts sand, two parts loam and one part peat, at 2-in. spacing.

EYE PROPAGATION: WISTARIA

Below—This is done in a heated greenhouse in late winter whilst the buds are still dormant. Slice the buds ("eyes") away from the parent shoot with 1 in. of the shoot attached and to half the thickness of the parent shoot.

Above—Lay the eyes flat, cut surface downwards and spaced 1 in. apart, in a 5-in. pot. Use a sandy mixture as compost. Press the eyes firmly into the compost.

Below—Surface the pot with ¼ in. of sharp sand after the eyes have been laid in position. Water with care and stand the pot in a propagating frame in a temperature of 65°–70°F.

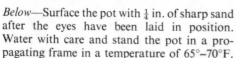

Above—An alternative method of eye propagation is to retain the full thickness of the shoot, but to cut to a length of about 1½ in. and insert the eyes firmly in an upright position. The same rooting conditions as mentioned above are necessary.

LEAF CUTTINGS: PEPEROMIA

Left—The large, well-developed leaves of this plant are suitable for propagation, rooting fairly readily in a greenhouse in spring or summer.

Right—Cut off the leaves and cut the stalk through cleanly with a sharp knife so that about 1 in. of stem remains.

Left—Insert the cutting firmly in a small pot so that the leaf base rests on the surface of the compost.

Right—Three leaf cuttings can be inserted in a 3½-in. pot. A suitable compost is half peat and half sand.

LEAF CUTTINGS: BEGONIA REX

Left—These thick, rather fleshy leaves can be cut into 1-in. squares and laid, underside downwards, on the shaded surface of a compost in a seed tray.

Right—Roots are formed at the edges of the leaf squares and later young plants develop, as seen here. Not all the leaf cuttings develop equally, and some are ready to pot on before others.

Left—A large leaf pegged down flat on the surface of a seed tray with wire hair pins. The thick "ribs" on the underside of the leaf are partially cut with a sharp knife at 2-in. intervals.

TAKING ROOT CUTTINGS

Below—Herbaceous plants with fleshy roots like eryngium, papaver and brunnera lend themselves to propagation by root cuttings. Lift the parent plant in winter and detach a stout root.

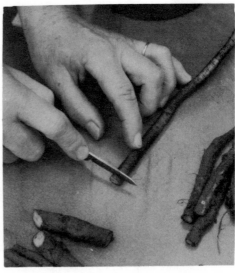

Above—Cut through the thickest end, i.e. the portion which was nearest the parent crown. Use a sharp knife and leave a flat surface.

Below—Cut through the other end slantingly to differentiate between top and bottom of the cutting.

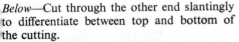

Above—The prepared cutting ready for planting should be about 2 in. long. Several such cuttings can be taken from each length of root.

INSERTING ROOT CUTTINGS

Left—Insert the prepared cuttings in a pot containing a mixture of 3 parts loam, 2 parts peat and 1 part sand. This should be fairly firm and surfaced with ¼ in. of sharp sand.

Right—Insert the cuttings so that the flat (top) surface is uppermost. Tops of the cuttings should be level with the surface of the compost. Insert the cuttings firmly, 1 in. apart.

Left—Cover the pot with a sheet of glass to encourage quicker rooting, and stand in a cold frame or a cold greenhouse for the winter months.

Right—New growths will develop on the top surface of the cuttings so that each cutting becomes a new plant and can be planted out in spring.

ROOT CUTTINGS IN A SAND BOX

Below—Prepare a wall of sand in a seed box by means of a wooden batten cut to the same measurement as the inside width of the tray. Lay a row of cuttings against the sand wall.

Above—Prepare another wall with the wooden batten.

Below—Cover in the cuttings by pushing the sand into place.

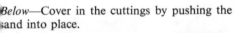

Above—The wall of sand ready for the next row of cuttings. Continue in this way until the box is filled.

ROOT CUTTINGS FROM PERENNIAL PHLOX

Right—Root cuttings of this type of phlox should be taken when young plants free from stem eelworm are required. (This pest causes a blackening of the lower leaves and severely stunts growth.) Take roots in winter when the plants are dormant.

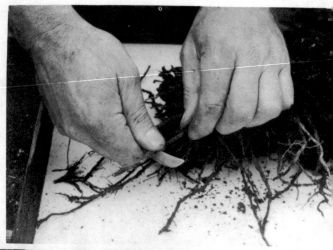

Left—Take cuttings 2–3 in in length and lay them fla on the surface of som sandy compost in a po or seed tray.

Right—Cover the cuttings with ½ in. of sandy compost and place them in a cold frame or cold greenhouse. New shoots will be made in spring, and the young plants can be set in a seed tray to grow on for 4–5 weeks before being planted out of doors in a reserve plot until autumn, when they can be planted where they are required to flower the following year.

METHODS OF DIVISION

Above left—Large tough clumps may be lifted, laid on a firm surface and divided by using two forks, drawing the handles together. *Above right*—Thick tufted clumps difficult to lift should be halved and then quartered *in situ* with a sharp lawn edging tool or spade; the smaller pieces can be moved without strain. Choose pieces from the outside for replanting.

Above—Simple division can be effected by lifting a portion from the side of a plant with a trowel. The best time to do this is early spring when new growth is about to start. *Left*—Plants with thick fleshy roots can be divided by cutting through the centre of the crown with a sharp knife. Each portion of top growth must have a section of root.

Right—Very large clumps should be cut into two equal pieces with a sharp edging tool or a spade with a sharp blade.

DIVIDING PAEONIES

Left—Li... the clum... carefully with all the roots intact, taking ca... not to damage the "eyes". Divide in March... September.

Left—Where the divided pieces are each 6– in. or more across, they may be divided again Paeonies do not take to being disturbed an should be divided only when the crowns ar very large.

Right—When planting paeonies, do not cover the tops of the crowns with more than 2 in. of soil, otherwise flowering may be delayed. The line indicates correct soil level.

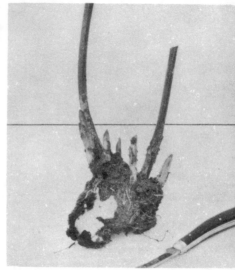

DIVIDING MICHAELMAS DAISIES

Right—Each portion so divided can in turn be pulled apart to make two further divisions.

Left—Lift and divide clumps in autumn or spring by pulling apart two equal portions.

Left—Michaelmas daisy crowns of both tall and dwarf varieties can be divided several times.

Right—A single rooted portion may be planted separately to form a new plant. Best results are obtained by this method of division, which can be done every other year.

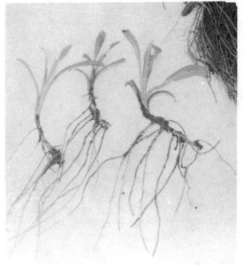

DIVIDING IRISES

Left—Division of the Bearded (June flowering) iris may be done in March, but more usually after flowering in August or early September. Divide overcrowded clumps to improve the quality of the flowers. A lifted rhizome ready for division is shown here.

Right—Cut off separate portions of the rhizome from the parent clump. Use the outer, younger portions and discard soft and old pieces.

Left—Each separated portion should have roots attached. Division can be continued down to single pieces, so long as each has some root.

Right—Cut back tops of the leaves and trim basal portions of the rhizome neatly with a sharp knife. Replant shallowly so that the top of the rhizome remains exposed.

DIVIDING POLYANTHUS PRIMULAS

Left—Lift the clump after flowering in spring and shake off the soil so that the root mass is exposed. Division is best done in dull weather when the soil is damp. *Below*—Pull the clump into pieces by gentle pressure of the fingers. Polyanthus lends itself readily to division, each parent plant giving up to 6–8 pieces.

DIVIDING SEDUM AND GEUM

Below left—A clump of *Sedum spectabile* of a size which can be readily divided. Many herbaceous plants give better quality flowers if divided every 2–3 years. *Below right*—A lifted clump of geum. Divide into two or more pieces by cutting the rather woody crown with a sharp knife. After cutting, pull the portions apart to obtain the young outside pieces.

BUDDING ROSES: PREPARATION OF ROOT STOCK

Left—Bush roses are budded on to root stocks, usually *Rose canina*, forming the root portion. When the bud grows, the top part of the root stock is cut off

Right—Prepare a trench 9 in. deep so that the roots can be laid in. Plant stocks in winter at 1-ft spacing to give sufficient working space when budding.

Left—After planting, firm the soil evenly around the stocks. If more than one row is being planted, space the rows at 2 ft apart.

Right—The base of the root stock when the soil has been removed, showing the portion where the bud is inserted in June. The original soil level is indicated by a line.

BUDDING ROSES: TAKING THE BUD

Left—Take buds from young shoots cut from flowering bushes in June or July. The shoots should be stood in water until required.

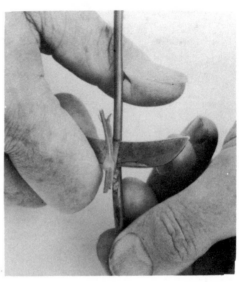

Right—Remove leaves but not leaf stalks. Detach the buds by slicing beneath them with a sharp knife. Use only stout, well-formed buds.

Left—A detached bud. A young shoot may have six or more buds, and all can be used.

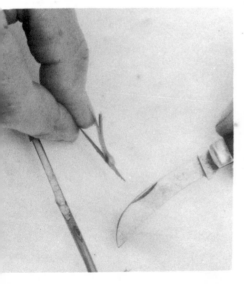

Right—Remove the sliver of wood at the back of the bud cleanly. The intact leaf stalk forms a convenient handle.

BUDDING ROSES: INSERTING THE BUD

Left—Make a T cut in the stock at the lowest point possible, after removing 1–2 in. of soil from around the base of the stem. If the bud is inserted higher up, suckers may result later on.

Right—Form the top of the T first, then make a downward cut about $1\frac{1}{4}$ in. in length.

Left—Open up the lips of the T with the handle of the budding knife to allow for easy insertion of the bud.

Right—Insert the bud into the T cut. Leave the leaf stalk—this will rot away after the bud has taken.

BUDDING ROSES:
TYING IN THE BUD

Below—A very convenient and quick method of securing the bud is to use thin rubber patches with two thin wire spikes.

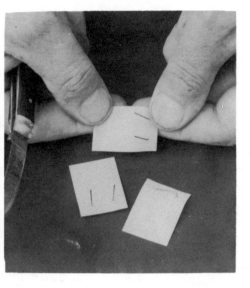

Above—Place the patch in position over the bud and secure by the wire spikes. The patch should be left in place to rot away.

Below—An alternative method is to use moist wide raffia. Bind around the bud above and below.

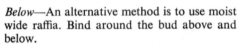

Above—Tying completed above and below the bud. When growth from the bud starts in spring, slit the raffia to release it. Cut off the portion of the root stock above the inserted bud in spring.

LAYERING BORDER CARNATIONS

Left—Use shoots on the outside of the clump for layering. Strip off the lower leaves on the shoots to be used. Several shoots can be layered from the same parent clump.   *Below*—With a sharp knife make a slanting downward cut about 1 in. in length into the underside of the selected shoot, to about the centre of the shoot.

Below left—Peg down the base of the layered shoot into a sandy compost, using bent wire. *Below right*—Cover the layered shoots with 2 in. of sand or sandy compost. Layer in July or early August and detach rooted layers from the parent plant the following spring.

LAYERING CLEMATIS INTO A POT

Right—Select a low growing shoot on the outside of the plant, which can be laid down near soil level. Layer in June or early July.

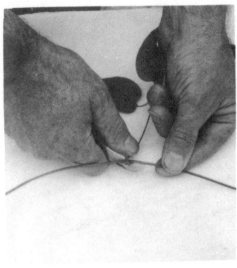

Left—Cut a slanting slit in the stem and set a 5-in. pot filled with a compost of three parts sand, one part loam and one part peat just beneath the point of cutting.

Below—Secure the portion bearing the cut with wire hair pins, so that it is set firmly in contact with the compost in the pot.

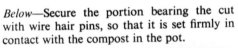

Above—Cover the layer with compost. Roots will form at the portion of the stem which is partially cut. Sever rooted layers in spring. More than one shoot can be layered from the same plant.

AIR LAYERING

Left—A method by which some woody subjects can be made to produce roots. Remove a few leaves and a strip of bark, then slide a polythene sleeve over the selected shoot.

Right—Treat the cut stem with rooting powder. Position the polythene sleeve and tie the base firmly in place.

Left—Pack damp moss all round the stem inside the polythene bag, ensuring that the stem is in the centre of the moss.

Right—Tie the top end, forming an airtight bag. Leave this covering in place until the roots can be seen—then remove the bag, sever the stem and plant the rooted part carefully.

CUTTING BEGONIA TUBERS

Left—To increase your stock of a specially fine variety of tuberous begonia, cut the tubers into two portions when the new shoots are well developed in early spring, i.e. after growth has started. Cut the tubers in half cleanly to leave a new shoot and some root on each portion.

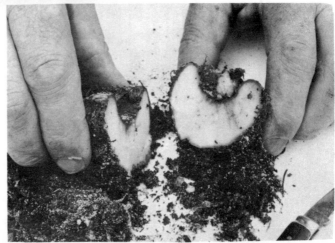

Right—It is essential that roots are left on each cut portion. Handle the cut tubers with care so that the roots are not broken or damaged.

Left—Pot each portion into a 3½-in. pot, using a compost of half peat and half J.I.P. 1. Do not pot too firmly. The top of the tuber should be level with the surface of the compost. Pot on to a 5-in. pot later, using J.I.P. 1 as compost.

GRAFTING CACTI

Left—Grafting cacti is worth trying when plants are available. With a sharp knife remove the top cleanly from the stock plant, which must be strong growing, and remove a piece of near matching from a slow growing variety.

Right—Place the matching piece carefully in position on the stock plant. As it is imperative that it does not move, place a piece of string with a lead weight each end over the top and allow to hang as shown.

Left—To form a vigorous Zygocactus (Christmas cactus), insert a leaf or scion into a slit made in a suitable stock. Pin in place with a cactus thorn.

Right—When the scion is in position, remove the top from the stock plant. This ensures that all nutriment goes to develop the new scion.

GREENHOUSES AND GREENHOUSE PLANTS

TYPES OF GREENHOUSE—1

Above left—A wooden greenhouse, size 10 ft 6 in. by 7 ft, available with or without staging. *Above right*—A cheap greenhouse made of Scandinavian softwood, size 8 ft by 5 ft. Available with or without staging.

Above—A wooden greenhouse, size 12 ft 6 in. by 8 ft 3 in. Optional staging (both sides) accounts for about one-sixth of its cost. *Left*—A wooden greenhouse, size 10 ft by 8 ft, for erection on a brick base. Optional staging (both sides) accounts for about one-fifth of its cost.

TYPES OF GREENHOUSE—2

Right—One of the most popular types of greenhouse, with low brick walls and part glass sides. It may be used for growing and raising a variety of plants, and staging can be fitted to one or both sides as required. *Below*—A polythene house is not usually heated, and is especially useful for spring and summer crops. If sectional it can be moved from one position to another.

Above—A lean-to greenhouse is often the most suitable type to construct. It should face south if possible, but a south-east or south-west position is suitable too. A lean-to may also be used as a sun lounge. *Left*—A greenhouse-and-shed combined is particularly useful where space is limited. The shed may be used for storage and/or as a potting shed. Extra protection is given if the shed is at the north end.

TYPES OF GREENHOUSE—3

Left—Some types of greenhouse can be purchased in section or in the separate pieces for erection by the purchaser. Here the uprights are being checked. *Below*—A Minibrite 8 ft × 8 standard aluminium alloy house erected and glazed ready for use. This one is on a wooden base, but brick or concrete is more usual. Note that maximum light is admitted in this type of house.

Below left—A concrete path provides a working area and makes for easier management. *Below right*—Note the hard working area outside the door of this house. Late chrysanthemums in pots following tomatoes is a popular sequence.

TYPES OF GREENHOUSE—4

Left—Oak and cedar are popular materials in use today for greenhouses. The Oakworth, a strong, rigid house, is a combination of wood with metal stays. Fix the ridge board on to the assembled side and roof sections.

ight—Next the stays, which are adjustable nd act as spacers between sections, are posi-oned and tightened, thus making the sections gid and ready for glazing.

Left—Glass, putty, brads and clips are provided together with the main parts of a house. Instructions for glazing are simple to follow. Ensure that the recommended lap-over for each pane is followed from the instructions.

ight—In trying to satisfy the different re-uirements of gardeners, manufacturers have day produced many variations of the green-ouse. This example has one half side of wood nd one complete side of glass.

HEATING

Left—A paraffin heater suitable for a small greenhouse. Several sizes and makes are available. This blue flame heater is economical to run and with no unpleasant smell.

Right—A convector can be used together with a tubular heater on very cold nights. Fitted with a thermostat, it comes on only when the temperature goes below the set figure.

Left—A fan heater with a built-in thermostat ensures that electricity is not wasted and an adequate heat level is maintained.

Right—Electrical tubular heaters are available in several sizes. Here a double tier is being used, but these heaters can be used singly or trebly as required. Doubles and trebles are controlled by a thermostat.

MORE ELECTRICAL EQUIPMENT

Right—Tubing and nozzles of an electrically controlled automatic watering system. Such a system, in which one nozzle is allowed per plant, enables an adequate amount of water to be continually supplied. *Below*—Where electricity is available, automatic pest control is provided by apparatus of this kind, in which the appropriate insecticide is vaporised.

Above—Lighting is an asset for winter work in the evenings and at week-ends. *Left*—A modern greenhouse fitted with a fan heater plus thermostat, an electrically heated frame and automatic ventilation.

MORE ELECTRICAL EQUIPMENT

Right — A greenhouse propagating frame which has two methods of heating: space heating by cables set around the sides of the metal case, and soil heating by cables in the soil. A frame of this type does away with the necessity of heating the whole house early in the year. *Below*— An Extractor Fan. One is sufficient for a small-to-medium greenhouse and is best positioned at the end of the house opposite the door.

Above—By removing the back plate a thermostat can be set at the required temperature so that the power is cut off when the predetermined temperature is reached. This ensures the most economical use of electricity. *Left*—A rod-type thermostat used in connection with greenhouse heaters, fans, soil and air temperature control.

HEAT RETENTION

Right—During cold spells in winter and early spring heat can be conserved by making a polythene tent over a batch of pot plants or seed boxes. This should be removed when the cold spell ends. *Below*—Newspaper also provides protection for seedlings during cold spells.

Above—In an unheated greenhouse, when a cold spell is expected in spring, extra protection can be given by lining the inside of the roof temporarily with newspaper. *Left*—Lining the inside of a greenhouse with heavy-gauge polythene sheeting can give 5–10 extra degrees of heat. Always line the ventilators separately to ensure adequate ventilation.

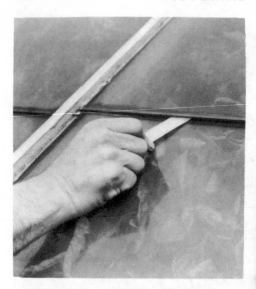

MAINTENANCE

Left—An example of poor glazing, causing cold draughts. Glass should overlap flush, so that both cold draughts and heat losses are prevented.

Right—Cleaning off loose paint from the outside woodwork before painting. Loose paint should be removed with a wire brush and then the woodwork rubbed down with coarse sandpaper.

Left—Cleaning down woodwork inside the greenhouse, using a wire brush. Painting is best done when the house is empty, as some plants are affected by paint fumes. Ideally, all inside woodwork should be repainted annually.

Right—It is important that glass should be kept clean so that maximum light is admitted, especially in winter and early spring. It is frequently necessary to wash the glass following fog.

VENTILATION

Right—Ventilation in the base walls can be provided by wire netting grills with sliding wooden covers which can be adjusted according to the ventilation needed. *Below*—Automatic ventilator units are available which open and shut according to changes in temperature. These are especially useful if the greenhouse is left untended for any length of time.

Above—Ventilation is especially important in a small greenhouse, and a hand-operated ventilator in the roof is the most usual method. The amount of ventilation is varied according to prevailing temperatures, but in summer, many crops need ventilation when the temperature exceeds 65° F. *Left*—Special ventilator bricks may be fitted when the base walls are being constructed, together with a wooden sliding cover inside the house to adjust the amount of "air" needed.

GREENHOUSE MANAGEMENT

Below—Temperature control is one of the basic factors in the management of a greenhouse. A good maximum and minimum thermometer is a valuable asset.

Above—Sturdy benches and/or shelves are essential. They make for easy work, especially where a wide range of pot plants is to be grown throughout the year.

Below—These pot plants are standing on a thick layer of sand in a specially constructed tray which is supplied with water from an upturned jar set at a lower level. Water is drawn up through the sand and drainage hole in the pot by capillarity.

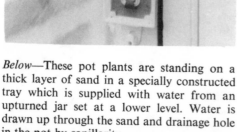

Above—One method of shading plants from spells of bright sunshine is to use the type of slatted roller blinds shown here.

SOIL STERILISATION

Above left—An electric soil steriliser filled with loam. Both potting and seed sowing composts should contain sterilised loam, which gives better growth and freedom from soil-borne diseases. Peat and sand are not sterilised. *Above right* — A special soil sterilising bucket with a water container at the base. The water is electrically heated and the steam passes up through the soil in the bucket.

Above—Formaldehyde can be used for chemical sterilisation. The treated soil is covered with sacks or polythene for 24 hours to keep the fumes in the loam. The covering is then removed and the loam spread out to disperse the fumes. Use a formaldehyde solution of 1 gallon to 49 gallons of water. *Right*—Any lumps in the sterilised loam are broken down before mixing with peat and sand to form seed-sowing or potting compost.

STERILISING BORDERS

Left—Clean soil is essential in the greenhouse border. When the house is empty, dig over the border thoroughly and soak with water to enable the liquid chemical to penetrate easily.

Right—The amount of chemical needed per square yard should be calculated from the instructions. Measure off the amount required to a given quantity of water, and mix thoroughly in a plastic or galvanised container.

Left—Apply evenly with a rosed can over a marked area. After treating the soil, shut all air vents and lock the door, leaving the house shut for 3 weeks. Open up after this period and ventilate for 1 week before returning plants.

Right—When the soil has been treated, the remainder of the house should be attended to. Brush down brickwork and wash all woodwork thoroughly with disinfectant. Finish off by cleaning the glass.

FUMIGATION

Above left—Several different methods can be used, but always check that the particular fumigant it is planned to use is applicable to *all* the plants in the greenhouse. Here Nicotine shreds are about to be ignited: these give off a dense smoke which kills aphids very effectively. *Above right*—Smoke-type fumigants are available in many sizes, to treat a given cubic capacity. Always ensure that the correct dosage is given.

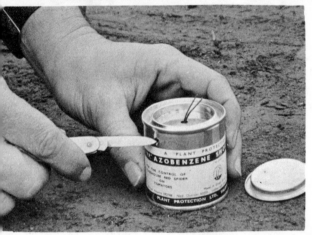

Above—Some fumigants and smokes are contained in metal canisters with side holes ready for puncturing. The wick ignites the contents of the tin, which is then forced out of the side holes as smoke. *Right*—When the greenhouse is empty, in autumn and winter, a sulphur candle may be burned. This is a good method to use after a tomato or cucumber crop where pests like red spider were troublesome. Burn the candles at ground level and stand them on an old slate or tile.

TOMATOES

Left—Useful crops of tomatoes can be grown in 10-in.-deep boxes on a bench in the greenhouse, using J.I.P. 1 as compost. Watering needs careful attention.

Right—With border on each side and brick support wall in front, plants can be set directly in the border soil. Ensure that drainage from the border soil is adequate.

Left—Tomatoes under glass in 10-in. whalehide pots of J.I.P. 1. Watering and liquid feeding is effected through the trickle irrigation lines.

Right—Tomatoes grown by the ring culture method in bottomless 9-in. whalehide rings stood on a layer of weathered ashes and ballast contained in trays.

CUCUMBERS—1

Right—Plants are raised by sowing singly in 3-in. pots. When they reach the stage shown by the plant on the right, they can be potted on to a 5-in. pot (left). The compost should be only lightly firmed. *Below*—Making up a bed 18 in. wide at the base, 12 in. wide at the top and 12–15 in. high. Plants are set 20 in. apart. They should be staked at the stage reached here.

Below left—When only one or two plants can be grown, set each on a mound of mixture made up of half manure and half loam. If neither is available, use J.I.P. 1, 2. *Below right*—Tying in the main stem to a supporting cane. This should be done regularly—almost daily when plants are growing freely. Pinch off any tendrils as they develop.

CUCUMBERS—2 *Left*—Apply a top dressing to the bed as roots show through, and repeat 2–3 times. Add 2 in. of fresh compost each time. Use the same material as for making the beds, but leave it in the house overnight to warm before use.

Right—Fruits develop on the laterals which are trained out along the wires. Laterals should be stopped (growing points removed) when two leaf joints are made. Stop further growths —"sub-laterals"—at one leaf joint.

Left—Lettuce and broad beans can be grown in 4–6 in. of soil on a bench or staging in a greenhouse—a method of special value in early spring. A variety like May Queen can be grown in an unheated house.

Right—Lettuce and radish being grown together in boxes stood on the greenhouse bench. The boxes can be easily removed when the crop has finished. The radish is ready to use before the lettuce is fully developed.

POTTED CHRYSANTHEMUMS—I

Left—Re-potting a late variety from a 5-in. to a 10-in. pot. Use J.I.P. 1 or 3 parts turfy loam, 1 part rotted manure and 1 part coarse sand.

Right—A plant established in a 10-in. pot. Note the amount of space left for watering. When the plant has become settled after potting—allow three or four days for this—remove the growing point.

Left—As a result of taking out the growing point ("stopping"), four or five shoots develop. These are the start of the main stems which will grow from this stage onwards.

Right—"Breaks" (see page 224) which have arisen from earlier stopping. The strongest shoots are retained. With some varieties, these shoots are stopped again, and the two best resulting breaks retained for flowering.

POTTED CHRYSANTHEMUMS—2

Below—Feed with fertiliser mixture every ten days. A suitable dressing is equal parts sulphate of ammonia and sulphate of potash.

Above—Disbudding is necessary so as to leave one main central bud at the end of each main stem. Remove unwanted buds when small, or as soon as they can be handled.

Below—All the main stems should be staked and tied securely. This ensures that the flowers are spaced and displayed to best advantage.

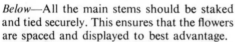

Above—Each main stem is tied in to a cane, allowing about an inch between the stem and the stake. The last tie should be made near the top of the cane to prevent damage to the flower heads.

POTTED CHRYSANTHEMUMS

—3   *Above Left* — Another method of staking chrysanthemums is to set three canes in the pot and tie fillis string around these to contain all the main shoots. Two or three ties may be needed as growth progresses. *Above right—* These plants grown in 10-in. whalehide pots stand on a polythene base which prevents weeds. Support canes tied to the wire above give protection against wind.

Above—Weeds, which may arise if unsterilised loam is used, should be removed from the base of the plant. Any unwanted basal chrysanthemum shoots at soil level should also be removed at this stage. *Left—* A hard path or area is best for pots to stand on outdoors unless polythene is used. In the case of plants that have been left standing on a soil base, soil should be scraped from the bases of the pots when they are brought inside the greenhouse in September. Drainage holes should be clear.

BEDDING PLANTS

Left—A wide range of bedding plants can be raised from seed sown in a heated greenhouse in February and March and pricked out into pots or boxes. Here sixty seedlings of Lobelia have been pricked out into a seed tray. *Below*—These asters are more widely spaced as only a small batch of plants is required.

Below left—Bedding plants can also be grown in pots. Three plants in a 3-in. pot can be grown on and the whole planted out intact. Larger plants are obtained by this method. *Below right*—Antirrhinums being "stopped", i.e. growing points removed to encourage the production of side growths. The latter process is known as "breaking". If plants are not stopped, they will flower sooner than stopped plants but will have one main central flowering stem only with the first flush of flowers.

POTTING *SANSEVIERIA*

Below—To remove the plant from its pot, knock the edge of the pot on the corner of a bench, holding the plant firm with the other hand.

Above—Set the plant in the centre of the new pot, which should be well crocked, with about an inch of compost over the crocks. J.I.P. 1 is a suitable mixture.

Below—Firm the compost with a label, filling in as necessary. Fairly firm potting is needed for sansevieria.

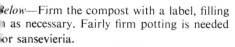

Above—Finish off by firming with the fingers or thumbs and leave the surface level. Allow sufficient space for watering. In a 5-in. pot, a space of $\frac{3}{4}$ in. is adequate.

POTTING ON—I

Left—To remove a plant from its pot, first tap the rim of the pot on the edge of a bench, holding the plant as shown.

Right—The ball of soil can now be taken out intact. When the ball is filled with roots the plant is ready for repotting.

Left—Crocks being placed in the bottom of a pot to cover the drainage hole, keeping it clear of soil and allowing free drainage. Adequate crocking is essential, and clean pots are best.

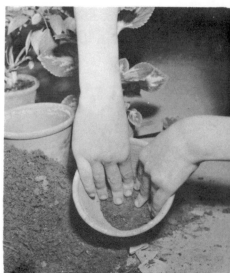

Right—Compost being placed over the crocks in the bottom of the pot before the ball of soil is set in place.

OTTING ON—2   *Below*—Place the
                plant   in   the
entre of the pot and stand it upright. Set it
rmly on the soil covering the crocks. Water
ants before potting on.

Above—Filling in with compost. Keep the
plant upright and central whilst this is being
done.

Below—Firm with a ramming stick where firm
otting is needed, and especially if large pots
re being used. Coleus, seen in this picture,
eed moderately firm potting.

Above—Finally, firm the compost evenly by
finger pressure. When potting plants on from
one pot to another, do not use too large a pot.
Move a plant from a $3\frac{1}{2}$-in. pot to a 5-in.
one, or from a $4\frac{1}{2}$-in. to a 6-in.

CARE OF POT PLANTS—I

Left—Washing the foliage of a Rubber Plant (Ficus) with a soft sponge to remove dust and freshen up the appearance of the plant. This should be done once every 3–4 weeks. Both sides of the leaves should be sponged.

Right—Potting a Pteris fern which has been divided by gently breaking the ball of roots into two or three pieces. This is best carried out in spring.

Left—For early flowering in a greenhouse most H.T. and Floribunda roses can be potted into 10-in. pots in autumn. Roots may need to be trimmed and carefully spaced in the pots.

Right—Roses need fairly firm potting and a rammer can be used for this purpose. A suitable compost is 3 parts loam, 2 parts peat and 1 part coarse sand (by bulk). The pots should be taken into the greenhouse in early winter.

CARE OF POT PLANTS—2

Left—As an aid to even watering, and to lessen work, place in a saucer a quantity of gravel chippings. Level the chippings on the saucer, firming them so that they are compact, and make an even surface for the pot to stand on.

Right—Water so that the water level comes up to the top of the chippings. Topping up is required every few days.

Left—Stand the pot plant level on the chippings. Water is drawn up through the moist gravel from below. This is a useful method to adopt when plants have to be left unattended for a few days.

CYCLAMEN—1

Right—If plants are being kept from one season to the next, they should be kept dry for 5-6 weeks in June-July but watered again when fresh growth starts in late summer. Plants can be re-potted when new shoots show clearly, or alternatively the top 2 in. of compost in each pot can be replaced, as shown here. *Below* — Plants making fresh growth in late summer in a cold frame. Move into the green-house in late September and feed with a liquid fertiliser.

Above—If young plants are to be raised from seed, sowing is usually in August and the seedlings are pricked out into 3-in pots. By the following spring plants can be moved on to 5-in pots as shown here. *Left*—The corm should be just showing through the surface of the compost when potting is finished. J.I.P. 2 is a suitable compost for these plants.

CYCLAMEN—2

Left—Washing the foliage with a soft sponge to prevent dust settling. Use tepid, not warm water for this purpose.

Right—Stirring the surface of the compost with a small fork after it has set hard will encourage fresh root production and allow free passage of water.

Left—Adding fresh J.I.P. 2 compost to the surface. Firm moderately. The corm can be at least half covered by the compost.

Right—Washing the pot to remove dirt and green slime. The surface of a pot should be scrubbed clean. Always wash pots thoroughly before using.

GERANIUMS

Above left—Geraniums which have been used for bedding should be lifted when frost threatens, and the soft tops cut back to about half way. These tops can be trimmed and made into cuttings. *Above right*—The cut back plants should be stood close together in a box with a light, sandy compost packed fairly tightly around the roots, and kept in dry, frost-proof conditions during winter.

Above—Plants can also be kept in pots during winter, and should be cut back to encourage fresh shoots in spring. This prevents the plants from becoming leggy. *Left*—In spring, place cuttings taken in autumn and potted up singly into 3–in. pots in a position near the glass so as to receive plenty of light. In winter, keep the plants dry and in frost-free conditions on bench or staging.

LILY OF THE VALLEY
AND FREESIAS

Left—A useful display of scented Lily of the Valley can be obtained in late winter and early spring by lifting roots and growing them in pots in a warm greenhouse. Use plump growths.

Right—Set the selected roots in a 5-in. pot using J.I.P. 1 as compost. Pot the roots fairly firmly so that the tops of the growths just show through the surface.

Left—For scented, colourful freesias in winter set corms in 5-in. pots in J.I.P. 1, in late August. Plant five or six to a pot, so that the tips of the corms just show through the surface. Keep in cold greenhouse conditions.

Right—When the foliage is 7–8 in. high, provide support by thin twiggy stakes. Keep the plants in a warm greenhouse from September onwards. Flowers will be produced from December.

HYDRANGEAS

Left—A young plant kept under glass starts new growth in early spring, and the old stem is best shortened back to a good new growth. If the surface of the soil is hard, loosen with a label.

Right—The same plant as above, shortened back to a strong growth and with surface soil loosened. About one inch of fresh potting compost has been added to the surface.

Left—On an established plant kept in a greenhouse new growth will start to develop in early spring. The main shoots should be shortened back to good buds, and thin unwanted shoots removed.

Right—The same plant as above, after shoots have been reduced in height by a quarter and dead wood removed. When the side growths on the lower part of the main stems are 3 in. long they can be used as cuttings.

FUCHSIAS

Left—When cuttings are established after potting on, the growing points must be "stopped" by pinching out with finger and thumb.

Right—As a result of stopping, shoots will be produced after a week or so from the axil of the leaf joint, giving a plant with three or four breaks and a bushy appearance.

Left—Where standards or half standards are to be grown, a stake should be placed in position early on to ensure that the stem is kept straight. Tie the stem every 6–8 in. and remove side shoots.

Right—On the left is a standard which is still being grown on; the growing point has not yet been removed. The half standard on the right has produced side shoots or breaks after stopping, so forming a flowering head.

TUBEROUS
BEGONIAS

Right— Tuber should be set flat surface upwards. The remains of the flower stalk can be seen in the right-hand tuber, which has the typical pronounced depression. On the left-hand tuber the old roots can be seen. *Below*—Tubers start growth at a temperature of just under 55° F, i.e. in February or March in the greenhouse. Place them in a seed tray prepared with peat or potting compost kept just damp.

Above—Set the tubers in compost or peat so that the tops are very nearly level with the surface. They should be settled firmly in and placed a fingerwidth apart. *Left*—When tubers have produced a good top leaf growth and roots have developed, each one should be potted singly in 3½-in. pots in J.I.P. 1. Firm the compost only moderately to prevent damage to the brittle roots.

GLOXINIAS   *Right*—These colourful summer greenhouse subjects can be started into growth in 3½-in. pots in a heated greenhouse in early spring. Use only firm tubers. Slight pressure with the fingers will tell whether they are sound.   *Below*—Set the tubers singly in the pots, which should be large enough to allow about 1 in. of clear space around the tubers. Damp peat is the best starting medium and the tuber should have the top just exposed.

Above—With the commencement of growth and the formation of leaves, the roots will be growing into the peat. This is the stage for moving on into J.I.P. 1 in the "flowering" pot. *Left*—Tubers can also be started in a seed tray and potted up singly at the stage shown here. Take care to avoid damage to roots and foliage.

IVY   *Below*—Ivy is easy to grow indoors. Where plants need repotting, a mixture of half sand and half J.I.P. 1 is suitable. Loosen the surface of the old ball of compost before repotting.

Above—Use a label to firm the fresh compost, then press with thumbs or fingers to obtain the final firmness and level. Sufficient space must be left for watering; in a 5-in. pot about $\frac{3}{4}$ in. is adequate.

Below—This type of plastic support allows growth to be trained neatly. Main shoots are tied in, and some of the longest shoots can be allowed to trail for display.

Above—Tying in the longest shoots to the supports. The main growths are trained outwards to keep the fan-shaped appearance and to prevent tangling.

OME UNUSUAL OT PLANTS

ight—Lachenalias are especi-
ly useful for spring flowering.
ulbs should be planted in
ugust, ½ in. deep and five to a
-in. pot. A suitable compost
J.I.P. 2. *Below*—Lithops or
iving Stones, so called because
ey resemble smooth, rounded
ebbles. These subjects are not
ifficult to grow. They should
e kept dry in winter and given
ery little water in autumn, but
atered fairly freely at other
mes.

Below left—The Sensitive Plant
(*Mimosa pudica*), the foliage
of which folds up when touched.
Plants can be raised from seed
sown in early spring, and grown
in 4-in. pots. *Below right*—
Calamondin (*Citrus mitis*), a
close relative of the orange, has
sweet-smelling, white flowers like
orange blossom, but is grown
mainly for its colourful, decorative fruits.

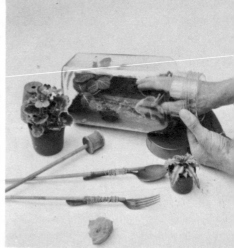

PREPARING A BOTTLE GARDEN

Above left—Numerous small plants can be grown in bottles and jars. Soil placing and planting can be assisted by a fork and spoon attached to canes. A sweet jar is a suitable container. *Above right*—Put a ½-in. layer of gravel into the container to ensure drainage, then sterilised compost to the required depth (about ⅓ full) and sloping towards the back of the jar. Keep smaller plants in front.

Above—On completion of planting, ensure that the plants are firm and that no roots are left uncovered. During planting soil will have become deposited on the leaves and sides of the jar: this can be washed off by syringing. *Left*—Bottle gardens are simple to maintain, the plants requiring very little attention. Foliage plants which do not flower are most suitable and will require no watering or feeding if kept airtight. Condensation, which may form in the morning, will clear when the room temperature rises.

CACTI AND SUCCULENTS—1

Below—Cacti and succulents are best kept in a greenhouse by themselves for ease of management, and must have frost-free conditions in winter.

Above—Cacti and succulents require very little attention. At the end of winter a very little water should be given. Compost set hard should be loosened and the top replaced with fresh.

Below—Adding fresh compost. A suitable mixture is 2 parts loam, 2 parts coarse grit, 1 part sand and 1 part peat (by bulk). A mixture of half J.I.P. 1 and half sand can also be used and gives good results.

Above—Gravel chippings give a pleasing finish to larger pots of cacti, and help to give drier conditions around the neck of the plant. Such chippings need to be one layer thick.

CACTI AND SUCCULENTS—2

Below—Treatment for mealy bugs found present on cacti. First enclose the pot and neck of the plant in polythene to prevent excess moisture and insecticide reaching the soil.

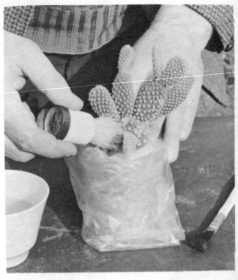

Above—Make up a weak solution of a suitable insecticide and brush over the plant thoroughly using an old shaving brush.

Below—Where cacti have crevices, and unusual growth, a small paint-brush enables all crevices to be reached.

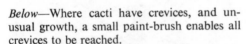

Above—After a suitable period of time to allow the insecticide to take effect, wash off the plant with fresh water. This may be sprayed from a small plastic container, ensuring that all crevices and corners are treated.

PREPARING TO PLANT BULBS IN BOWLS

Right — Where bowls with no drainage holes are being used, put a piece of charcoal in the bottom. This is not essential with pots or bowls having drainage holes. *Below*—Bulb fibre should be well wetted before use. If it is used dry, it is very difficult to keep moist later on. Surplus water should be squeezed out before using, leaving it moist but not sodden.

Above—Firm and level the fibre in the bottom of the bowl in which the bulbs are to be set. *Left*—Adjust the amount of fibre placed in the bottom of the bowls so that the tips of the bulbs will be just above the level of the rim, and just show through the final level of bulb fibre.

PLANTING BULBS IN BOWLS

Right—Hyacinth bulbs can be set four in a 7-in. bowl, spaced 3 in. apart, with the tips just showing above the surface. Make certain that the bulbs are set firmly, and that adequate space is left for watering. *Below*—Narcissi being planted five in a 7-in. bowl. Irrespective of the size of bowl, the bulbs can be set so that they nearly touch. Depth of planting should be the same as for hyacinths.

Above—Tulips should be spaced out at least 1 in. apart, better still 2 in. Depth and firmness of planting as hyacinths and narcissi. *Left*—Three bulb subjects for early flowering—narcissi, tulips and hyacinths. A wide range of varieties is available in each case. After planting, the bowls should be placed in a dark cupboard or plunged out of doors, in order that a good root system is formed before the bowls are brought back indoors.

CROCUS CORMS

Left—Special crocus bowls allow for a maximum display of colour. Corms are planted as the bowls are filled. One corm can be placed at each hole.

Right—Set some corms on the surface of the fibre as well as by the holes. At the top, corms can be set touching to give a maximum flower effect.

Left—When growth has begun, move the bowls into full light and keep in cool conditions. If kept in a very warm room crocuses may not flower, making ample foliage at the expense of flowers.

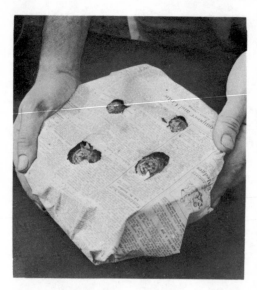

TREATMENT OF BULBS
AFTER PLANTING
Left — Afte
planting, th
bowls should be covered with newspaper fc
protection before being plunged out of doors.

Right—A small batch of bowls plunged.
Cover with about an inch of peat to ensure
that the bowls lift cleanly (this is an alternative to using newspaper as shown left). Next
cover the peat with 5 in. of soil or fine ashes.

Left—Brushing loose soil or bulb fibre fron
around the new growths after taking out of th
plunge bed. Take care not to damage th
growths. If the bowls have been kept in a dar.
cupboard, bring them out into the light.

Right—Where roots have grown through the
holes in the sides of crocus bowls, remove
them cleanly.

AFTER-CARE OF HYACINTHS

Left—When hyacinths are brought into the light or taken from the plunge bed, lightly stir the surface of the compost to enable easier watering and encourage root growth.

Right—To forward a backward growth or a bud which is slower to develop than the rest, cover with a small pot. This should be left in place for ten days.

Left—Moss being added to the surface of a bowl of hyacinths. This gives a more natural appearance. Bowls of narcissi or tulips can be treated in the same way.

Right—Tall spikes of hyacinths need a thin stake to support them. This should be set behind the spikes. Tie neatly with thin green illis string. Canes should not be quite as tall as the flower spikes.

CARE OF NARCISSI

Left—Tall-growing varieties need support and one method is to use thin canes. These should not exceed the height of the foliage. Tie in the leaves with thin raffia or string.

Right—Another method of support is by thin twiggy shoots of elm, hazel or similar wood. Push these in firmly between the growths.

Left—Trim back the unwanted stakes and space out the flower stems by resting them against a suitable piece of twig. Aim at having the flowers well spaced out to give a maximum display.

Right—Covering the surface of the compost in the bowl or pot makes an attractive finish and enhances the appearance of flowers and foliage.

VEGETABLES

DIGGING AIDS

Left—The basis of digging — a stout pair of boots, a good clean spade and an upright stance. Dig only for short periods, then have a change of job or a rest before continuing.

Right—Using a motor cultivator with revolving blades to prepare the soil for sowing or planting. There is a wide range of cultivators available, many costing less than £100. Such machines take much of the labour out of soil cultivation.

Left—Terrex spade. Push into soil until foot rest touches soil and handle slopes. *Right*—With foot still on rest, pull handles back just far enough to loosen spit. Remove foot from rest and pull handle back and down: the spade automatically lifts and turns spit.

SINGLE DIGGING

Left— Divide plot into two equal parts. Start at A and work from A to B. Move soil from first trench at A to D where it will be used to fill in the last trench. When A to B has been dug, fill in last trench at B with soil from first trench at C. Then dig from C to D.

Right—Compost being brought to the plot before digging is started. It will be spread evenly and incorporated into each trench as digging proceeds. A useful dressing is a barrow-load to every two square yards. Farmyard manure is a good alternative to compost—if it is in short supply, use what is available.

Left—Half the plot has already been dug (A to B), and the other half (C to D—see top of page) is now being dealt with. Compost is being added to each trench and not spread over the whole plot first. Spread the compost or farmyard manure evenly in the bottom of each trench. Note the box for perennial weed roots, which should be taken out as digging proceeds.

DOUBLE DIGGING

Below— Manure being added to the 2-ft-wide trench and dug in. This ensures that the soil is dug to the depth of two spits—about 18 in. or twice the depth of the spade blade. Part of the garden can be so treated each year for special crops.

*Above—*The next 2-ft-wide strip being dug and soil thrown forward to cover the strip shown in the previous photograph. Half the 2-ft-wide strip is being dug, to be followed by the other half. When this is completed, the bottom of the trench is dealt with.

*Right—*Trenching is for very deep rooted vegetables or when crops are being grown for exhibition. Soil is dug to depth of two spits and third spit forked, soil being kept at its original levels. Here second spit (A) is being dug over to same level as first trench. It will be covered by soil from C after bottom of trench has been forked up.

RIDGING AND ROUGH DIGGING

Left—Ridges left rough to obtain the maximum effect of weathering in winter. This is of especial benefit on a heavy soil and should be done as early in winter as possible. *Below*—"Rough" digging, i.e. where the soil is dug to the depth of one "spit" (the depth of a spade blade). Here the spits are being turned over roughly to obtain maximum winter exposure.

DRAINAGE

Above— On heavy soils and on those where drainage is poor, 4-in.-diameter land drains can be set on a layer of ashes. The trench is 1 ft wide; the depth will vary according to the nature of the soil, but should be about 2 ft to avoid disturbance. A slight slope is needed to carry off the water to the lowest point. *Right*—Leaf mould or strawy compost when dug in will aid drainage and help to lighten heavy soil. It also adds useful organic material.

LIMING

Right—Even distribution of lime is ensured by weighing out the required amount for the number of square yards to be dressed. 4 oz. per sq. yd of hydrated lime is often applicable under average conditions, but the level of acidity—the *p*H reading—is the best guide. *Below*—Lime is not applied every year to the whole of the ground, but some crops benefit from a dressing each year, e.g. runner beans, so apply lime to the area intended for them.

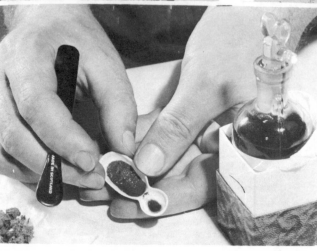

Above—A simple test for presence of lime can be carried out by pouring hydrochloric acid on a small quantity of soil. If lime is present, the acid will cause "fizzing". If the soil has no free lime, there will be no reaction. Such a test does not determine the *amount* of lime in the soil. *Left*—A soil testing outfit determines the level of acidity or alkalinity—"*p*H value"—thus showing the amount of lime needed.

PREPARATION
OF SEEDBEDS

Above—Ground which was dug in the autumn becomes compacted during the winter. When intended for a seedbed it should first be forked over lightly to a depth of 6 in. and the lumps broken down with the tines of the fork. *Right*—Make sure that all the plot is trodden evenly. This will break down any remaining lumps and contribute to the final tilth.

Left—Finally, rake the plot using an iron rake. Stones and hard lumps of soil should be removed. A dressing of superphosphate at 4 oz. per sq. yd should be raked in before seeds are sown. This ensures good root formation, which is the basis of success with small seedlings and young plants. Where a brassica seedbed is being prepared, also add 4 oz. of hydrated lime per sq. yd.

Above—"Drills" for small seeds are best drawn with the corner of a hoe. A garden line keeps the drill straight, and depth may be varied according to seeds sown. Draw the drill to an even depth, otherwise germination will vary.

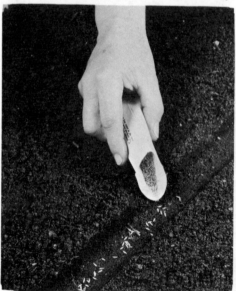

Above—Small seeds are best sown direct from the packet; sow as thinly and evenly as possible. *Right*—The larger seeds—dwarf beans, etc.—can be sown by hand according to the recommended spacing.

SOWING

Above—A 5-in.-wide drill being drawn for peas—it would also be suitable for broad beans. Standing on a plank avoids uneven soil consolidation. The drill should be drawn to an even depth for the whole of its length.

AIDS TO GERMINATION

Right—Where peas or broad beans are to be sown in a 4- or 6-in.-wide drill, a layer of peat lightly worked into the bottom will give greater moisture retention and better germination. Alternatively, the drill can be surfaced with a 1-in. layer of peat. *Below*—Lawn mowings placed over the drills after sowing serve as a mulch to conserve moisture, and also to give some protection from birds.

Below left—Slow germination is often caused by dry soil. Watering drills before seeds are sown ensures even and rapid germination. Flood large drills, using the can without the rose, but for small drills keep the rose on the watering can. *Below right*—Shading a small seedbed with planks. This gives cool, moist conditions and helps the germination of many small biennial flower seeds sown in May or June. Planks should be removed as soon as germination is apparent.

THINNING SEEDLINGS

Left—Thin lettuces s that only one plant left at each statio Thinning is easie when soil is dam and there is least di turbance when weath is dull and rain thre tens. Thin the see lings as soon as the are large enough to b conveniently handle

Near right—A small hand hoe, often called an "onion hoe", is useful for the initial thinning to leave the seedlings in clumps. Take out the smallest plants. *Far right*— After the initial thinning the plants are left in small groups. The final thinning is done by hand to leave the best plant at each site at about 8-in. spacing.

Far left—Beetroot seed lings are first thinne to leave a single row This is best done whe the plants are abou 2 in. high. *Near left*— For the main crop i.e. for storage, plant should be thinned s that they are 3–4 in apart.

PLANTING PERMANENT CROPS

Below—Preparing sites for rhubarb at 3-ft spacing. This crop will benefit from a generous dressing of farmyard manure or compost, which should be dug in before planting.

Above—Set rhubarb crowns so that the buds or eyes are just above soil level. Large established clumps can be divided if necessary, but each division must have at least one eye.

Below—Asparagus, showing the position which should be adopted for planting the crowns in spring. Note the well-spread roots.

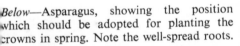

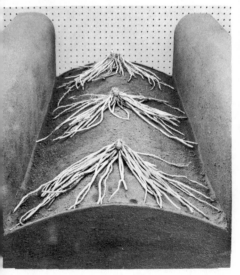

Above—Horseradish is planted so that the tips of the roots are just above soil level. Pieces of root 1 ft long are suitable, and should be set about 1 ft apart.

PLANTING ONIONS, HERBS AND MINT

Above—Planting Welsh onions in small clumps 1 ft apart. Set the plants firmly about 3 in. deep. This is a useful type of onion for salad and general flavouring.

Below—Dividing a clump of chives for further planting at 1-ft spacing. Chives are a mild-flavoured form of perennial onion, useful for salads, and are easily grown in most soils. Often used as an edging.

Below— One sage plant is usually enough for household purposes. Choose a sunny position in well-drained soil.

Above—Mint roots being laid flat on the soil surface before being covered with 2 in. of soil. The pieces are 3–4 in. long. Plant in early spring.

FORCING CHICORY

Right— Preparing chicory roots for forcing. The top growths are cut back to 3–4 in. *Below*—Trim the side roots back flush with the main root.

Below left—Packing the prepared roots close together in 10-in. pots. The root portion is set firmly in light and well-drained compost. *Below right*— After planting, give dark conditions by covering with an inverted pot of the same size and place in the greenhouse.

FORCING SEAKALE

Left—A seakale root being dug out in readiness for forcing in batches from November to January. Lift the root intact as far as possible. *Below—* The main roots are used for forcing. The thin side roots can be kept for planting where a further stock of plants is required.

Above—Roots prepared and trimmed for forcing in large pots or boxes. *Right*—Seakale roots being placed in a deep box after trimming. Pack some old potting compost between the crowns. Keep in dark conditions at a temperature of 55° to 60° F and water regularly. Force in batches to give a regular supply from November to January.

FORCING RHUBARB

Left — Early rhubarb can be obtained from the greenhouse by placing the crowns under the staging in dark conditions in December or January. Lift the crowns 2–3 weeks before this time and leave them out of doors in frosty weather if possible. Then stand them close together under the staging with soil between them. *Below*—All eyes in each crown should be sound, and soft tissue cut away.

Below left—Small batches of rhubarb can be forced by placing a crown in a bucket on rotted manure. Keep in dark conditions in a greenhouse—if heated, growth will be more rapid. *Below right*—Out of doors, earlier rhubarb can be obtained by covering the crowns with a wooden bin, large bucket or tall drainpipe to give dark conditions and so draw the shoots up more quickly.

FORCING POTATOES AND BEANS

Right—For early potatoes from the greenhouse, set one tuber to a 9-in. and two to a 12-in. pot of light, well-drained, rich compost. Half-fill the pot with compost and set tuber of an early variety in the centre. Cover with a 3-in. layer and add more as growth develops.

Left—Add more compost to the pot when the potato shoots are 4–5 in. high to encourage further development of roots and tubers.

Right—Green beans are grown specially for their shoots. Seeds are sown thickly on a damp piece of sacking which is kept in warm conditions. The shoots —an essential ingredient of many Chinese dishes—are cut when they are 4–5 in. long.

FORCING TURNIPS, MUSTARD AND CRESS

Right—Turnip tops being cut from stored roots. A seedtray can be used for forcing, the aim being to produce fresh green leaves for use in salads or for cooking. *Below*—Place tops, cut surface downwards, flat on compost in a seedtray. Press lightly into soil surface and cover with an inverted seedtray to give dark conditions. Growth is quickest in a heated greenhouse.

Above—Forcing mustard and cress indoors. A piece of sacking is first cut to the size of the seedtray. *Left*—Seed is sown thickly and evenly on the sacking which should be kept damp and covered with an inverted seedtray to exclude light until the seedlings are 3–4 in. high. Growth will be quickest in a warm greenhouse.

PREPARATION OF FERTILISERS AND LIQUID FEEDS

Right—Fertilisers must have all lumps broken down before the dressing is applied. If this is not done, application may be un-even or excessive. *Below*—Stone jars make useful storage containers. Always store ferti-lisers in a dry place. In damp conditions they may become sticky or set in hard lumps.

Above—One method of making a liquid feed is to place a bucket-ful of animal manure in a bag and suspend this in a tub of 20 gallons of water. A thick concentrated liquid is obtained after a few days which can be diluted down to the strength required. *Left*—Measuring off the required amount of a pro-prietary liquid feed to add to a known quantity of water accord-ing to the maker's directions. Never be tempted to use too strong a concentration.

FEEDING

Right — Beans will benefit from a side dressing of a complete granular fertiliser at ... oz. to each yard run of row, applied down one side of the row. Such dressings should be hoed in, and are best given in dull damp weather or when rain threatens.

Left—Onions. Hoeing in a top dressing, using a Dutch hoe. Onions respond to a dressing of complete fertiliser at 2 oz. per sq. yd, applied to the soil between the rows. Give this every 10 days whilst growth is being made.

Right—Outdoor tomatoes appreciate a liquid feed with a high potash content. Such liquid feeds should be applied every 10 days. This regular feeding, plus watering, will ensure that the fruit will not crack or split, which often happens when rain or heavy watering follows a prolonged dry spell.

FEEDING AND MULCHING

Below—Making holes with a dibber close to leek plants. This allows easier liquid feeding with manure water or proprietary liquid feeds, which is essential for the growth of really fine specimens.

Below—Runner beans may be mulched with lawn mowings to help retain soil moisture—an important point with this crop. A mulch about 1 in. thick is ample. Repeat as the original dressing rots down and shrinks.

Above—Mulching around rhubarb crown with strawy manure. Compost can be used a an alternative. In either case, a generous laye 3–4 in. thick should be used.

Above—Outdoor tomatoes may be mulched when the plants are 2 ft high. Here lawn mow ings are being used. Rotted manure or com post is better still. Dry soil can lead to frui cracking or splitting.

CELERY DISEASES

Left—Celery leaf spot in a sharp attack can severely affect leaves and check growth. Spray with a copper fungicide at the first signs of attack, and repeat two or three times at intervals of 10–14 days.

Right—Celery fly. Marks and channels are used by larvae feeding in the leaf tissues. Spraying with a malathion preparation is effective, whilst dusting the foliage with BHC will kill the adult flies and prevent egg laying.

Left—When spraying plants apply the insecticide at a good pressure and cover both surfaces of the affected leaves. If a dust is used, apply when the plants are damp to obtain a good coverage.

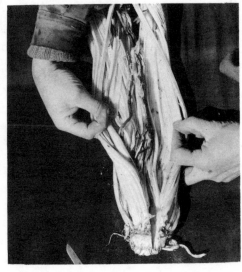

Right—Soft rot of celery can be caused by over feeding with nitrogenous fertilisers, too heavy organic manuring with insufficient potash or by soil trickling into the hearts of the plants. Worst in a wet season when growth is soft.

POTATO DISEASES

Above—Potato blight can cause total loss of foliage if the disease is unchecked. Tubers may be damaged, though the rot may not show until storage. Most troublesome in wet summers.

Above—Spraying with a copper fungicide protect plants against blight. Wet upper ar lower leaf surfaces thoroughly. Apply sever times in a wet season.

Above left—Corky scab. See commo scab (below) for control measure *Above right*—Wart disease. Ther are many immune varieties of potatoe and these should be planted if th disease is known to be present. *Left*—Common scab is most severe on soi low in organic matter, or on gritt ashy garden soils. Add peat, gra mowings, compost or farmyard manu to the open drills at planting time, c dig in before planting when tube are set on the flat. Do not apply lin to ground intended for potatoes.

TOMATO DISEASES

Left—One of the worst troubles of outdoor tomatoes, especially in a wet summer, is blight. This disease affects both foliage and fruit, which is spoiled by a black rot. Spraying with a copper fungicide is the best control, either before symptoms appear or at the first signs of attack.

Right—Plants need to be sprayed against pests, particularly aphids, and the type of pressure sprayer shown here is very effective.

Left—Verticillium wilt. Affected plants flag by day and revive at night, when not short of water. Treat the border soil in winter, when the greenhouse is empty, with a chemical soil steriliser. *Right* —Split fruit may be caused by the outer skin becoming hard in a dry spell. After heavy rain or heavy watering the skin ruptures. Aim at even watering throughout the season.

BRASSICA DISEASES

Left—Cabbage root fly larvae can kill outright or severely check a high percentage of a cauliflower crop. Damaged plants wilt in fine weather.

Above right—Club root affects all brassicas. Dress infected soil when uncropped with hydrated lime at 8 oz./sq. yd. *Below*—Also: dip roots in a paste made of 1 lb. 4 per cent calomel dust in $\frac{1}{3}$ pint water just before planting.

Above—Dusting around the base of a brassica plant with lindane within 3–4 days of planting will give protection against cabbage root fly.

PEST CONTROL

Right—The larvae of the cabbage white butterfly and similar pests can quickly cause considerable damage and even strip the plants of leaves if no control measures are taken. Dust with BHC, derris or pyrethrum at the first signs of damage. *Below*—Black bean aphis can be checked by spraying the plants with malathion or derris. In either case, spray as soon as the aphids are seen, and before they increase in numbers.

Above right—Pinch out the tips of broad beans where black bean aphids are present at an early stage of the attack. This "stopping" not only gets rid of the pest, but helps quicken the development of the bean pods. *Right*—Cabbage gall weevil also causes swellings and lumps on swedes and on the roots of many other brassica plants. The same control measures as are taken against the cabbage root fly are effective. Where this pest is anticipated, mix a small amount of lindane with the seed at sowing time.

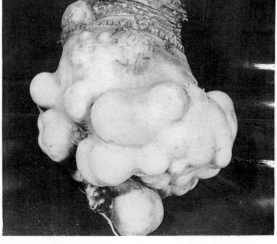

PEST CONTROL

Left—Damage to carrots and other root crops from wireworm can be prevented by applying Gamma BHC to the site before sowing, using 1 oz. per sq. yd. Apply the dust evenly and hoe it into the top few inches of soil. *Below*—Applying Gamma BHC alongside rows for hoeing into the top few inches of soil to kill onion fly.

Above—Hoeing in lindane dust alongside rows against carrot fly. The Gamma BHC soil treatment which is described above for use against worm is also effective here. *Right*—The pea and bean weevil causes damage that can be seen most easily at the edges of the leaves, giving a scalloped appearance. Dusting the plants with derris at the first signs of attack will give an effective control.

EST CONTROL

Below — Close attention should e paid to slug control, especially in dull, damp eather. Lettuce are particularly prone to ttack. Slug bait or pellets should be placed ear the plants.

Below—Flea beetle damages brassica seed-ings by eating holes in the leaves. Affected plants should be dusted with derris powder t the first sign of attack. Here radish are being treated.

Above—Wireworm is often a pest in garden soil which was recently grassland. Dusting the soil lightly with BHC before planting or sowing gives a good control. Here pieces of carrot used as traps are being buried near infected plants.

Above—Dusting alongside a row of carrots with lindane in early May to kill adult carrot flies, thus preventing egg laying. Repeat in late July to prevent a second brood.

MORE PROTECTIVE MEASURES

Right—Damage to small seedlings is often caused by birds dusting in dry soil. Newly sown seeds can be protected against this by being covered with pea sticks, which should be laid in position fairly thickly along rows. *Below*—Celery should be protected against possible prolonged rain in autumn. Stiff corrugated paper can be bent over and kept in place above the plants by canes.

Above—Small plants are easily damaged by cold winds. One form of protection is short sticks or pea stick material set about 6 in. away from the plants on each side. *Left*—Beet should be protected at night, when frost threatens, in early autumn. Fix stout string or wire just above the foliage and suspend newspaper from it.

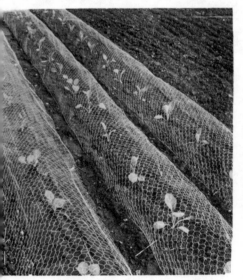

Right—Protect bean plants late in the season when frosts threaten. Here some old curtain material is being used. The coverings should be removed next day when the temperature has risen above freezing.

Right—Outdoor tomato plants can be protected from cold winds and full advantage taken of any sunshine by setting cloches on edge on the north side of the plants.

MORE PROTECTIVE MEASURES

Left—Bending over the leaves nearest the curd will help to protect cauliflowers in winter from frost and prolonged wet spells. Leaves will bend without snapping if handled carefully.

Left—Where birds are known to be troublesome brassica rows can be protected by using ½-in. mesh wire netting. Rows of peas can be treated in the same way.

ASPARAGUS AND BROAD BEANS

Left—Apply a top-dressing of a complete fertiliser to asparagus to encourage growth in summer after cutting of shoots has ceased. Such a feed encourages development of the crowns and so ensures increased production of shoots for cutting the following spring. *Below*—Support growths in late summer where a single row of asparagus is being grown. This is the best method of cultivation for a small area.

Below left—Remove basal shoots of broad bean plants from the main stems. *Below right*—Support broad beans with canes and stout string to prevent them from being blown down and damaged by winds or heavy rain. Push the canes firmly into the soil.

RUNNER BEANS

Above left—Stout stakes make the best supports for runner beans and should be pushed firmly into the soil after the seeds are sown or when the plants are showing. Better quality beans are obtained from staked plants. *Above right*—String fixed to wires or poles at top and bottom makes a good support. Upright stakes at intervals are necessary to take the weight of the plants on the string.

Above—Take out tips of main shoots when the beans reach the tops of the stakes. This gives better flower setting. *Left*—A good method of watering roots on light soils is to sink a drainpipe into the soil alongside the plants.

CELERY

Above left— Celery plants can be raised in boxes from seed sown under glass in February or early March. Harden them off and set out of doors in April or early May. When taking plants from boxes keep roots intact as far as possible. *Above right—* Planting in a trench in a single row at 9-in. spacing. Where space is limited set two rows 1 ft apart in a trench 18 in. wide. Use the space between trenches for a fast growing intercrop such as lettuce.

*Above—*One method of blanching celery is to cover the stalks with paper collars or thick newspaper. Side shoots arising from the base of the plants should be removed first. Tie paper or collars firmly in position. *Left—*When using paper or collars draw up the soil to aid blanching. Take care that no soil falls between the stalks—if this happens the centre of the sticks may rot.

BRASSICAS

Left—Brassicas are best set in a shallow drill to make watering more effective. Plant so that the lower leaves just rest on the soil surface.

Right—Water in dry weather and after planting. If damage from larvae of the cabbage root fly is anticipated, water with a lindane solution within four days of planting.

Left—All brassica crops will benefit from a top-dressing of a nitrogenous fertiliser such as sulphate of ammonia applied at 1 oz. per sq. yd. Such a dressing should always be hoed in.

Right—Draw the soil up close to spring cabbage plants in autumn to give extra protection from severe weather. This also helps to give better drainage on a heavy soil.

LEEKS

Above left—Leek plants should be set 1 ft apart in holes 6 in. deep made with a dibber. Drop the plants into the holes and do not fill in with soil. A mark on the dibber ensures that all the holes are made to an even depth. Trim off the ends of leaves and long roots before planting. *Above right*—Plants being watered in to prevent any check after planting. Note the trimmed leaves.

Above—The holes are finally filled in by hoeing. The stem is blanched by the covering of soil. *Left*—Keep the soil hoed up to the developing stems in late summer and early autumn to help blanching. Large plants may be grown in a single row in a trench and earthed up in the same way as celery.

Right—Set the plants out of doors at 9-in. spacing. Here a near-by row of cloches gives some protection from wind.

LETTUCE

Left—Remove lettuce plants from seedtray in March for planting out after hardening off. Handle plants by the leaves—never stems, which may cause damage and subsequent rotting off.

Left—Depth of planting is important: lower leaves should be just above soil. Later batches may be sown at intervals from March onwards where they are to mature.

Right—Tie up cos—two ties—to give a better heart. Here raffia is being used but rubber bands are also suitable.

MARROWS

Right— Marrows may be grown on a heap of soil or a mixture of half soil and half compost. Farmyard manure or compost alone usually gives over-soft growth. *Below—*To assist pollination and fruit production, transfer pollen from the male flowers to the stigma (central portion) of the female flowers. The latter are distinguished by the small embryo fruit at the base of the flower where the male flowers have only a thin stalk.

*Above—*Cut back ends of main shoots to encourage a better set of fruit. This will also help the fruit to fill out. Do not permit side shoots to develop if the fruit is already set. *Left—*Some protection from wet conditions and slug damage can be given by placing a sheet of glass, piece of slate or thin board beneath each fruit. Raise this off the ground by placing it on bricks.

MUSHROOMS

Left—Mushrooms can be easily grown in trays or boxes using one of the composts specially sold for the purpose. The compost must be evenly damp but not wet, and should be well firmed down and allowed to settle.

Right—Here brick-type pawn, which stores quite well, is being set in small pieces—about walnut-size —just below the surface of the compost. The tray is then stood in a warm shed or cellar.

Left — Pick mushrooms when ready by twisting gently so that none of the stem is left behind. Care should be exercised so as not to break off the small ones whilst picking those that are ready.

ONIONS

Below—Onion sets should be planted 6 in. apart in a shallow V-shaped drill in March. Set the bulbs firmly. This method of growing onions is much easier than raising them from seed.

Above—Cover the sets by raking soil into the drill until the tips of the bulbs just show through the surface.

Below—Spring-sown onions in rows 1 ft apart from a March sowing. Hoe frequently in the early stages to keep down weeds. Spring-sown onions need not be thinned when only small to medium-sized bulbs are required.

Above—Flower stems should be pinched out when small, otherwise the plants will "bolt", i.e. produce flower heads, preventing proper bulb formation. Take care not to loosen the bulb when removing flower stems.

PEAS

Left — Bushy, twiggy sticks, approximately the same height as the variety being grown, are often used to support peas. Set the sticks firmly in position when the plants are 3 in. high. They can be placed upright or at an angle.

Right—An alternative method of support is to use wire netting of the appropriate height, placed at one side of the row only. Keep the netting firm and upright by using canes at intervals.

Left—A well-grown row of peas in full flower. Large weeds must be removed from the base of the row by hand. A mulch of compost or decayed lawn mowings is beneficial at this stage of growth.

POTATOES—1

Right—Potatoes to be used for planting should be stood on end in trays in January or early February and kept in a light, frost-proof shed or building. The resulting sprouting or "chitting" ensures an earlier crop. *Below*—The eye or "rose" end from which the shoots emerge. This end of the tuber should be set uppermost in the tray.

Above—Well-sprouted, large-seed tubers should be cut in half lengthways. Each portion must have one or two sprouts. Such division should be done at planting time and the cut portions planted immediately. *Left*—Tubers will produce very many more sprouts than are required. If left on when the tubers are planted, they will slow up growth. Thin the sprouts so as to leave the best one, or at the most two.

Right—Give a top-dressing when the plants are 4–5 in. high just before the first earthing-up. Do not allow the fertiliser to fall on the foliage. Use a general fertiliser at 2 oz. per sq. yd.

POTATOES—2

Left—Tubers should be planted in rows 2ft apart, the drills having been taken out with a spade. For an early crop set the tubers 1 ft apart. Sprouted tubers ensure quicker progress and a more even crop.

Left—Fork between rows to ensure ample soil for earthing—made much easier when the soil is loose and friable.

Right—Earthing-up may need to be done two or three times. An early crop grown at closer than usual spacing, however, need not be earthed at all. Frequent attention to earthing is a good cultural factor on a new garden soil.

PARSNIPS

Below—When large, long parsnips are required, use an iron bar to make holes 2–2½ ft deep and 1 ft apart—a good method on a heavy soil, but the whole plot must be dug beforehand.

Above—Fill the holes with old potting compost. This should be made moderately firm and allowed to settle for a week or so before sowing.

Below—Sow two or three seeds at each station. When the seedlings are showing the first rough leaf, thin them out to leave the best plant at each station.

Above—Where parsnips are grown in drill drawn with a hoe for general purposes, thi the seedlings to leave the best ones standin at 5–6-in. spacing.

SHALLOTS *Right*— Plant bulbs in early spring 6 in. apart in rows 1 ft apart, setting them so that the tips just show above soil level.

Below—Development can be aided by hoeing away the soil from the base of the clump. A top-dressing of complete fertiliser at 2 oz. per sq. yd will be of benefit at this stage.

Above—Bulbs are nearing ripeness when the foliage dies down. Lift the clump intact and dry off in a sunny spot ready for storing. *Left*—Early shallots can be grown in pots set close together. Here 3½-in. pots are plunged into the soil to rim level. This is a useful method where space is limited.

TOMATOES

Left—Outdoor tomatoes should be planted in holes 15 in. apart. A warm sunny situation is best. Use of pot-grown plants ensures that there is no check in the early stages. *Below*—Plants may be set with a permanent polythene mulch. Holes are cut in the black sheeting to take the stems and leaves. Such a mulch is useful on a light soil as it slows down soil moisture loss.

Below left—Use a complete fertiliser before planting, at 4 oz. per sq. yd. This contains nitrogen, phosphates and potash. *Below right*—Tying after planting is important and further ties should be made as necessary. Tie the cane first, then the stem. Do not draw the plant too tightly to the cane—leave a space between stem and cane.

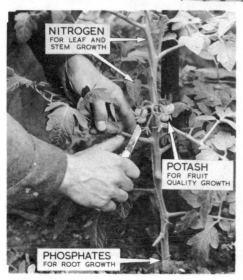

NITROGEN FOR LEAF AND STEM GROWTH

POTASH FOR FRUIT QUALITY GROWTH

PHOSPHATES FOR ROOT GROWTH

TOMATOES— RING CULTURE

Right—Digging a trench in which a 5-in. layer of ballast or weathered ashes is to be placed. The plants are grown in bottomless containers stood on the aggregate. *Below*—Lining the base of the trench with polythene before putting the aggregate in position. The base should slope so that water drains away easily.

Above—The containers should be two-thirds filled with J.I.P. 1 and the plants set in these. When the roots are well established in the aggregate, water and feed with liquid through the compost in the rings. The plants must be watered in the rings until roots are well developed in the aggregate. *Left*—Plants should be staked and tied regularly. Outdoor tomatoes do best in a sheltered sunny spot and in warm dry summers. Spraying against blight is necessary in a wet summer.

SHOW VEGETABLES

Right — Absence of blemish is all-important with white varieties of potato. A clean, well-matched sample, matched for both shape and size, has a good chance of being amongst the prize-winning exhibits. Always check that the correct number of tubers are shown. *Below*—Brussels sprouts need to be carefully trimmed and selected for evenness of shape and size. Each should be blemish-free, fresh and of good colour.

CAMBRIDGE SPECIAL

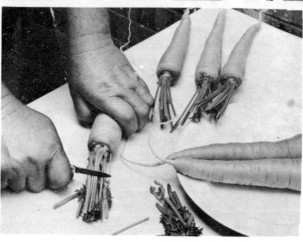

Above—Celery calls for the highest standard of cultivation to produce sticks of the kind shown here. Good length of blanched stalks is important, as well as general quality and absence of blemish or pest damage. *Left*—It is not always easy to select unblemished carrots for exhibition purposes, but a clean, evenly matched dish of roots should be aimed at. The tops can be shortened back as shown here just before staging.

STAGING EXHIBITS

Right—Beet for exhibition must be of even shape, not over-large, well matched and in a fresh state. The use of parsley as a "finish" is not permitted at all shows— always read the schedule carefully. *Below*—In some classes of peas a given number may be asked for. When handling the pods, avoid blemish to the "bloom" on the skins by handling as shown. Pods should be fresh, well filled, at the peak of condition and evenly matched for size.

Above—Shallot bulbs show to best advantage standing erect in a plate of dry sand or sawdust. Select bulbs for exhibition so that they match for shape and size as evenly as possible. *Left*— Onions are another example of the value of selecting even-sized specimens of good shape. Size is an important point. All bulbs must be well ripened ("well finished") and tops should be tied down neatly.

SELECTION OF SPECIMENS FOR SHOWING

Right— Selection for size, even shape and even stage of ripeness is well illustrated in these tomatoes. Avoid over-ripe fruits. Stalks should be left on and in a fresh condition. *Below* — Dwarf beans. Select straight pods of even length and width, and with stalks intact. The three specimens on the right are typical high-quality pods. Discard beans like those on the left.

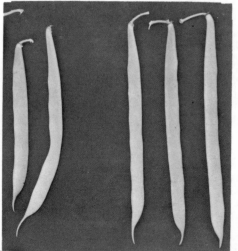

*Above—*Leeks of even size and high quality. A good length of blanched stem is essential for exhibition purposes. *Left—* Catriona potatoes, a popular choice for exhibition where a coloured kidney is required. Unblemished tubers should be chosen, as near matching in shape and size as possible.

SHOWING COLLECTIONS

Right—Different shows and different classes call for a varying number of vegetable kinds. Nine different vegetables are shown here, with cauliflower forming a centre-piece. *Below*—Very high quality is the first consideration, and celery, leeks and onions are often the basis of a collection.

Above—A well-balanced exhibit with the various kinds displayed to best advantage, carrots making a useful centre-piece. The selection of varieties for exhibition purposes is an important consideration, particularly for onions, carrots, potatoes, leeks and celery. *Left*—Note the liberal use of parsley as a garnish around the cauliflowers, thus showing off the white curds to advantage.

HARVESTING AND STORAGE

Left—Vegetables that have to be stored—carrots, beet and potatoes—may be kept in boxes in a dry frostproof shed. Onions can be hung up in ropes. All these crops should be dry when stored. *Below*—A shed to be used for storage can be made more frostproof by an extra layer of roofing felt.

Below left—Storage facilities are increased by shelves. *Below right*—Another method of storage, using a rack and shelves. Orange boxes make very useful storage containers for root vegetables.

MORE METHODS OF STORAGE

Right—The Dutch-type tomato tray, with wire netting base is suitable for storing roots, as it allows good air circulation.

Below—Small quantities of potatoes can be stored in sacks in a dry, cool, frostproof building.

Above—Clamping is a good method of out-door storage. The roots are layed in fine dry soil and covered with straw to give protection against frost. *Left*—The straw is then covered with a 6-in. layer of soil tapered at the top to allow water to run off. The site should be well drained.

STORING CARROTS

Left—Carrot tops should be cut off after lifting. The roots must be clean and dry for storage. Lift with a fork, taking care to avoid damage. *Below*—The roots should be set in layers in a wooden box (an orange box is very suitable) with sand or peat between the layers. Make sure that only sound roots are stored.

STORING BEET

Below left—Twisting off the tops, leaving about 2 in. of leaf stalk. This lessens bleeding, which occurs if the leaves are cut off. *Below right*—Beet may be stored in peat or sand in a deep box. The boxes must be kept in a dry, cool, frostproof building. Only sound roots should be stored.

STORING GARLIC AND ONIONS

Left—Garlic bulbs should be lifted in early autumn for storage or use as required. Only small amounts need be grown for ordinary household use.

Right—A bulb is made up of several portions ("cloves"). Each of these small portions is replanted separately in spring.

Bend over the tops of onions in late summer to hasten ripening.

A rope of onions as lifted. Store in a cool, dry place with tops on and avoid bruising.

To store, remove dry leaves and root-ends. Leave 4 in. of dry leaf to twist round rope.

STORING MARROWS, POTATOES AND SHALLOTS

Left—Marrows may be stored in straw in a dry, frostproof building in autumn. The fruits must be fully developed, sound and unblemished.

Right—Lifting potatoes for storage when the soil is fairly dry. Care should be taken to avoid damaging the tubers with the fork tines. Rub off large lumps of soil and leave the tubers on the soil surface to dry for a few hours after lifting.

Shallots can be ripened off under cloches after being lifted. Keep them in one layer and harvest when dry. Do not bruise the bulbs when handling them.

Shallots should be stored in dry, cool conditions in trays. Take off the dried outer skin, ends of roots and dried leaves.

CLOCHES AND FRAMES

TYPES OF CLOCHE

Left—The popular "barn" cloche. Extra height is obtained by standing the cloches on a line of bricks. Note the tightly stretched line to ensure a straight row.

Right—A plastic cloche—unbreakable and easy to erect.

Left—The EFF cloche. Note the method of ventilation.

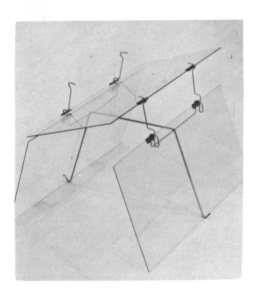

Right—A simple "tent" cloche suitable for low-growing crops can be made by using a clip and two sheets of glass, say 18 in. by 12 in.

METHODS OF USE

Left — Where seedlings are to be raised, draw drills. Early batches of vegetable plants can be sown in February or early March.

Right—If plants are being raised in pots, stand them close together to make full use of the space available.

Left—An early crop of peas or dwarf beans can be obtained by sowing and moving the cloches over the rows to give protection. Crops can also be grown alongside a row of cloches, thus making use of the shelter.

Right—Rows of seedlings may be raised under cloches. The ends of the rows are closed with a sheet of glass stood on edge and kept in place firmly with canes or thin stakes.

SOME CROPS
FOR CLOCHES—I

Right—Lettuce and onions to-gether. After the lettuce are cut the onions remain. Thinnings may be used for an early batch of salad (green) onions. An early batch of main crop onions can be obtained by sowing direct under the cloches in January or February. *Below*—Early carrots for pulling in June (variety Early Gem) may be sown with rows of early seedling brassicas between.

Above—Early lettuce spaced 8 in. apart for cutting in March and April when it is most in demand; note the slug bait in position. May Queen and May Princess are both popular and suitable varieties. *Left*—Early beet is a very suitable cloche crop, and may be grown in conjunction with early carrots. An early round variety is used for this purpose, the roots being pulled when of golf-ball size.

OME CROPS
OR CLOCHES—2

ight—Cucumbers planted in
May are a useful summer crop
or larger cloches. Telegraph is a
ood variety. *Below*—An early
crop of an early variety of potato
ke Di Vernon is always popu-
ur. This is a dwarf variety and
may be planted in late January
r early February using sprouted
eed.

Above—Spring cabbage planted
in October is always welcome in
severe weather in February and
March. Ellams Early is a suitable dwarf variety. *Left*—
Cloches can be used for an
early crop of strawberries.
Cloche the plants in December
or January and the protection
will ensure a good set of fruit
despite frosts, which can lead to
severe loss of blossom with
outdoor crops.

USE OF CLOCHES IN LATE SUMMER

Right—Although the main use of cloches is for early cropping, they may be put to other uses late in the season. Outdoor tomatoes can be laid down on straw in late July or early August to hasten development and ripening. *Below*—To hasten ripening still further, cut off all the tomato foliage to expose the fruit. In late summer cloches also protect against blight, which can be severe in a wet summer.

Above—Onions can be ripened off under suitably sized cloches in July or August—particularly necessary in a wet summer. Note the spaces left between the cloches for ventilation. *Left*—Bulbs being ripened off after lifting, suspended on a rail to give maximum air circulation.

Right—Early marrows, each being covered with a cloche to give protection in the first week or so after planting. The bush types of marrow are very suitable for an early crop.

Right—A batch of gladioli which were cloched earlier. The cloches have been removed and now protect another crop. Lettuce was grown between the earlier gladioli.

MORE USES OF CLOCHES

Left—Stand large cloches on end to protect tall plants like tomatoes. Stand cloches so that they give shelter on north, east and west sides.

Left—Melons, especially the Cantaloup varieties, are a useful summer crop. The fruits can be stood on an inverted pot or sheet of glass to help ripening and prevent slug damage.

VENTILATION OF CLOCHES

Below—Ventilation depends on type of cloche, crop and time of year. Here early beet is being ventilated by spacing the cloches a little wider apart.

Above—Where appropriate, a pane can be removed from the side of the row. Lettuce may become scorched in very warm spells, especially on dry soil—a condition to prevent.

Below—Tomatoes being given ventilation by removing the whole of one side of the row of cloches. This should be done by day, the glass being replaced in the evening.

Above—Strawberries being given ventilation on a very warm day in spring. The top glass may also be removed for weeding or any other attention.

PROTECTIVE
MEASURES WITH
CLOCHES *Right*—When it
is necessary to
hoe between plants, move only
one or two cloches at a time, re-
covering as the work proceeds.
Below—When frost threatens in
early spring give extra protection by clipping newspaper over
the tops of the cloches. This is
specially important if frost-
susceptible crops are being
grown, e.g. dwarf beans and
tomatoes.

Above—Soil drawn up to the
sides of the cloches prevents
draughts and raises the temperature in cold spring spells.
Left—Close attention to slug
control is important, especially
with lettuce. Here slug bait is
being set in place.

MAINTENANCE OF CLOCHES

Below—Glass should be kept clean at all times to allow maximum admission of light—especially important in early spring. Town areas produce more dirt than country.

Above—The ends of a row of cloches can be sealed off with a pane of glass stood upright and kept in place with a peg and wire.

Below—When a line of cloches are being placed in position, use a tightly stretched line to ensure a straight row. Soil must be level to ensure that the cloches all stand even and admit no draughts through cracks.

Above—When cloches are not in use, which will not be often in a well-managed garden, stand them on end. All glass should be cleaned before the cloches are used again.

TYPES OF FRAME—1

Right—A frame is particularly valuable for raising seedlings early in the year and for pot plants. A good size for use in a small or medium-sized garden is 4 ft by 3 ft.

Left—A metal frame of this type has the advantage of admitting the maximum amount of light. Extra height can be gained by resting the frame on bricks. This type requires the minimum of maintenance.

Right—A polythene frame is suitable for spring and summer use, especially for lettuce and flower and vegetable seedlings. It is light in weight, easily moved and cheap, but does not admit as much light as glass. Other more rigid glass substitutes are available.

TYPES OF FRAME—2

Right—A 6 ft-by-4 ft light being used as a temporary frame resting on turf sides and ends. This method is useful for temporary protection or short-term cropping. *Below*—Dutch lights. These have the advantage of admitting the maximum amount of light, but breakages are costly. The single-pane lights are usually 4 ft 11½ in. by 2 ft 7¾ in. They can rest on 10-in.-high back boards and 8-in.-high front boards.

Above—A double glazed polythene frame. One thickness of sheeting is used above and one below a light wooden framework. Such frames are useful for temporary protection, especially in spring. *Left*—A wooden frame of this type has the advantage of extra height and allows taller crops to be grown, although it can also be used for general purposes. It is easily portable.

HEATED FRAMES

Right—Low-voltage electrical soil-warming cable being laid. A frame thus fitted can be used as a hot bed for growing early crops or for raising seedlings early in the year. Note the staples holding the warming wire in position. *Below*—When the cable is placed in position it should be covered with at least 6 in. of soil. Full details of this type of installation can be obtained from electricity service centres.

Above—Where a frame with soil heating is used for raising plants, seeds can be sown in pots or boxes and placed on the soil layer. If they are covered with a sheet of glass, extra earliness and still quicker germination can be obtained. The uncovered cable is exposed for the purposes of this photograph. *Left*—"Space heating." Electric cable is laid round the inside edges of the frame, giving, in effect, a miniature greenhouse. A thermostat controls the temperature according to the weather and requirements of plants.

FRAME MANAGEMENT

Left—Where crops are to be grown directly in the frame, digging to the depth of the spade is necessary—particularly important with lettuce, carrots, marrows and early cauliflowers.

Right—When a frame has been used for several seasons the soil should be changed or treated with formaldehyde. Use the latter at 1 gallon per 49 gallons of water, or *pro rata*, and water on at 5 gallons of the solution per sq. yd. The frame must be empty during treatment.

Left—The treated soil is covered with old sacking for 48 hours and then forked through to disperse the fumes. This treatment is especially beneficial in tomato growing.

Right—Shading. In summer, crops like cucumbers and melons will benefit from a light shading in very bright weather. A thin solution of lime wash may be used, applied with a syringe or distemper brush. A thin coating only is needed.

VENTILATION OF FRAMES

Right—A block of wood cut in "steps" can be easily adjusted to provide varying amounts of ventilation.

Below—Flower pots of varying sizes can be used for the same purpose. Pots 3 in., 4 in. or 5 in. will provide the appropriate amount of ventilation needed at any given time.

Above—Another method of providing ventilation is by using a prop made from a length of wood which is fitted with cross slats (A and B). This type of prop allows crops to be attended to within the frame without the light having to be removed. A bracket (C) ensures that the prop will not be knocked away accidentally. *Left*—Polythene frames propped up to allow work on the lettuce crop beneath. Where this crop is grown for spring cutting very little ventilation is needed, except in warm weather in March.

EXTRA PROTECTION FOR FRAMES

Right—The temperature in a frame can be raised and maintained in winter and spring by piling manure or compost, or even straw, along the sides and ends up to the level of the top edge. *Below*—Some crops, like rhubarb or bulbs grown in pots and boxes, may be covered with a layer of straw. Plants being kept in the frame in winter, e.g. chrysanthemum stools, can also be protected in this way.

Above—Sacking or similar material provides a good covering in winter when frost is likely, and prevents draughts. In very severe weather sacks can be filled with straw to provide even more protection. *Left*—Where several frames have to be covered in winter, a roll of hessian is very suitable. This is quickly and easily placed in position. It should be weighted down at the ends and at intervals on top, especially in an exposed position. Remove when temperature is above freezing.

MAINTENANCE OF FRAMES

Left—Regular painting is essential where wooden frames are being used. Use white lead paint. Sound woodwork ensures no rotting or dripping.

Right—Where breakages occur, first remove all the broken glass and brush the woodwork with a wire brush to ensure that it is clean for taking the fresh putty. When inserting new glass, deal with woodwork in the same way.

Left—When the new glass is bedded down on the putty, it should be kept in place with sprigs or glazing brads. Clean the glass after insertion to remove finger marks or dust.

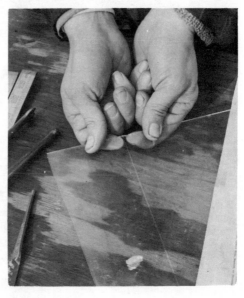

Right—To cut glass to size, lay flat on a level base and cut with a glass cutter along a straight edge on one side of glass only. Press or tap lightly on other side to give a clean break along line of cutting.

CROPS FOR FRAMES

Right—Several vegetables may be sown in a frame in February or early March: cabbage, cauliflower, Brussels sprouts, leeks and onions. One method is to mark off the frame and sow each variety in a square, either in shallow drills or thinly broadcast. *Below*—Cucumbers are a popular summer crop in a cold frame. Set one plant in the centre of the frame and train laterals into each corner. Note the shading on the glass

Above—Growing mushrooms in summer. Here grain-type spawn is being sown broadcast on the prepared surface in the frame. It is covered 2 in. deep, and the light is put on and covered with sacking to keep it dark. *Left*—One of the most popular and useful crops in a cold or heated frame is lettuce. The variety May Queen is very suitable for March cutting. Seed should be sown in October and the plants set out at 8-in. spacing in early January.

FRUIT

PLANTING A TREE—I

Right—A hole should be made large enough to take the roots well spread out. Remove the soil to a depth of 18 in. and heap it on one side; then loosen the soil at the bottom of the hole with a fork. *Below*—If the existing soil is very poor or very heavy, add some well-rotted compost to the planting hole. Always mulch newly planted fruit trees with peat or compost.

Above—Trees packed for transport often have their fine roots bent. Any broken or damaged roots should be trimmed with a knife, leaving a clean cut. *Left*—A tree must be staked to ensure that there is no movement to disturb the roots after growth begins. With the planting site and tree ready, place the stake in position and hammer in firmly to the depth required.

PLANTING A TREE—2

Right—Put the tree in the hole, ensuring that the previous planting depth, which can be seen on the stem, will not be exceeded when the soil has been replaced. Keep the stem of the tree as close to the stake as possible and spread out the roots evenly all round. *Below*— Some roots may be springy and not readily stay in position. They should be packed with soil to hold them firm before the filling in is continued.

Above—Fill in with soil as finely broken up as possible, and firm each layer in turn. This is best done with the foot— not too heavily. *Left*—The plastic strap and buckle is the best method of tying a tree to a stake, allowing adjustments to be made as the trunk thickens.

PLANTING CURRANTS

Left—The fine, fibrous roots of black, red, and white currants should be left intact, but the thick ones should be trimmed back before planting to lessen the likelihood of damage.

Right—As with all bushes and trees with good root formation, a sufficiently large hole must be prepared to ensure that there is no cramping of the root system. The roots should be spread out evenly and soil worked between and around them. With black currants, plant the bush slightly deeper than it was previously set.

Left—After planting a two-year-old black currant, cut each shoot back to leave only one or two buds at the base. Red currant bushes have a short stem and the main branches should be pruned initially by about half.

PLANTING GOOSEBERRIES

Below—Young gooseberry bush with a good head and length of stem ready for planting in winter. Two- or three-year-old bushes of this type quickly establish themselves.

Above—Note depth of planting, a short leg being left to keep the branches clear of soil level. This is important where bushes are to be spur pruned.

Right—Prune the bush after planting by shortening the branches to about half way, cutting to an outward-facing bud on each branch.

PLANTING STRAWBERRIES

Left—Well-rooted strawberry plants establish themselves quickly. Planting in early autumn gives forward plants the following spring. *Below*—Planting. Do not cramp the root; make a large hole with a trowel, not a dibber. Do not plant when the soil is wet.

Below left—Firm planting is essential, and the soil should be firmed evenly around the crowns to encourage fresh root formation. *Below right*—Depth of planting is important. The crown should be just above soil level. Fresh roots are made immediately above the existing ones.

PLANTING RASPBERRIES AND BLACKBERRIES

Left—Planting new raspberry canes in autumn. Canes should be spaced 15–18 in. apart, rows 6 ft apart. It is important to plant firmly.

Right—After planting cut the canes back to within 6 in. of soil level to encourage growth of new canes from the base in the season following planting.

Planting a blackberry. Note ample size of planting hole. Plant firmly and leave at least 10 ft between plants.

Cut back after planting to 6 in. Young loganberry canes should be treated in the same way, including planting distances.

PRUNING APPLES—I

Above left—Newly planted bush apple tree before pruning. Prune in winter whilst the buds are still dormant. *Above right*—After pruning. The main shoots have been shorted back, each to an outward facing bud to encourage an open appearance in the head of the tree.

Above—Five-year-old bush apple tree before pruning in winter.   *Left*—After pruning. Leaders are lightly pruned and laterals shortened back to 2–3 in. Prune similarly for next 5–10 years, "tipping" leaders less each year.

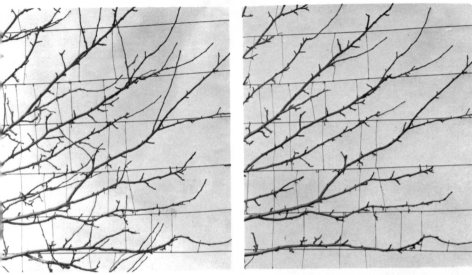

PRUNING APPLES—2

Above left—Fan trained tree before pruning. *Above right*—After pruning. Note leaders lightly tipped and laterals shortened back to 1 in. This method is applied only to fan trained apples and pears.

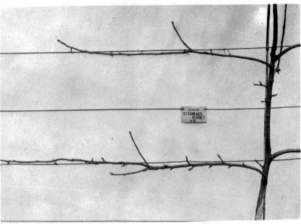

Above—Espalier before pruning. *Left*—Espalier after pruning. The ends of the main shoots have been tipped and laterals shortened back to 1 in. The leader, which is not shown, has been cut back by about one-third so that growth will be promoted from buds lower down on the leader from which the next branches can be selected.

PRUNING APPLES—3

Left—An established espalier apple before pruning. Note laterals.

Right—The same tree after pruning. Laterals have been cut back to two buds, except where fruit spurs have already formed. Prune in winter whilst the trees are dormant. An espalier pear is pruned in the same way.

PRUNING PLUMS

Left—An established half-standard plum needs very little pruning. Some of the thickest clusters of shoots should be thinned out in summer, but no hard cutting or shortening of shoots is needed.

PRUNING APPLES—4
(established trees)

Below—A bush apple tree branch before pruning. Note the appearance of the laterals. *Right*—The same branch after laterals have been shortened back ("spur pruning"). The leader (end of main branch) has been only lightly tipped.

Below left—Close-up of a spray before pruning, showing leader and laterals. *Below right*—Thinning out the fruit spurs. This reduces the number of fruit buds and thus increases fruit size, giving fewer but larger fruits.

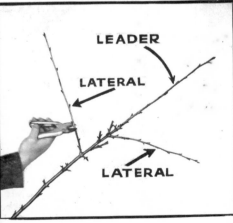

LEADER

LATERAL

LATERAL

PRUNING GOOSEBERRIES

Right—Established gooseberry bush in winter before pruning.

Below—After pruning. Laterals have been shortened back to 1 in. ("spur pruning"). This method is used where large berries are required. Note that the low-lying branches have been removed.

PRUNING RED CURRANTS

Below left—An established red currant bush in winter before pruning. *Below right*—After spur pruning, with leaders only tipped and all laterals shortened back to about 1 in. Fruit is borne on the old wood and on the bases of young shoots.

PRUNING BLACK CURRANTS

Above left—The first season's growth after a 2-year-old black currant bush has been planted and pruned. *Above right*—Pruning an established bush in winter by removing the older shoots and leaving in the young wood made the previous summer. The best fruit is borne on young wood.

Above—Take out a few of the thinnest young shoots at soil level to encourage new wood from or just below the point of cutting. *Left*—The bush after pruning. Some branches have been cut to near soil level to encourage the production of ample new growth, which is required each year.

PRUNING PEACHES

Right—Peach tree fan trained against a wall. Note that the centre of the tree is left open.

Below—Shoots are trained downward and outward. The uppermost shoot will be retained.

PRUNING GRAPES AND BLACKBERRIES

Above—A: Grape vine rod before pruning in winter. B: Rod with laterals cut away to leave one bud on each. C: Base of a lateral with the strongest bud breaking. *Left*—Blackberry canes, variety Himalayan Giant, trained to wires. Some of the older shoots are retained for fruiting.

SUMMER PRUNING

Below—Shorten back the laterals of apple and pear cordons and espaliers to about half way in July to restrict growth.

Above—A lateral after being shortened back to a leaf joint. Treat all laterals similarly.

Below—Black currants can be pruned immediately after the fruit has been picked in summer. Retain the young shoots.

Above—Gooseberries and red and white currants also benefit from summer pruning. Shorten the current year's laterals back by a half to two-thirds; next year's fruit will come from these.

Left—Cut back each branch in winter and graft in March. First cut a slit in the bark.

Right—Prepare the scion with a sloping cut 2½–3 in. long. Scions are shoots cut in winter, when dormant, and "heeled in" (planted in a cool place) until required.

Left—Insert each scion in a slit in the bark: two opposite each other in a branch 2–3 in. thick.

Right—After insertion tie round firmly with raffia to keep the scions secure.

RIND GRAFTING—2

Below— Cover the tied raffia with grafting wax, which may be cold or of a type which requires heating.

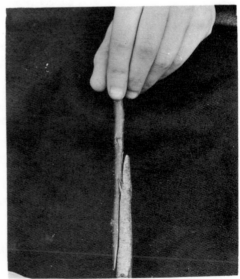

Above—The finished appearance of a bush tree which has been re-grafted or re-headed by the rind method.

Below—The scions unite with the branch at the point of union, and buds send out new shoots. Note that the raffia has been severed; this is done when growth is apparent—usually about a month after grafting.

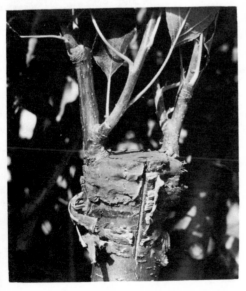

WHIP AND TONGUE GRAFTING

Used for stock and scion of similar thickness. A "tongue" secures scion, and raffia is bound round scion and stock and waxed over.

BUDDING

Right—Budding is a method used for the propagation of apples, pears, cherries and plums. It is done in June–July. First prepare a T-cut.

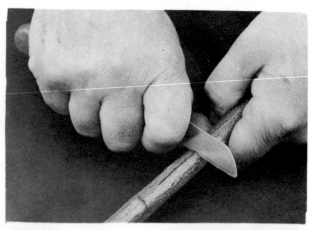

Below—Open the sides of the T-cut to facilitate insertion of the bud, using a knife handle.

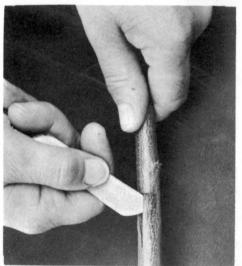

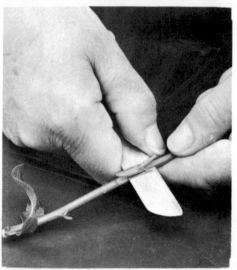

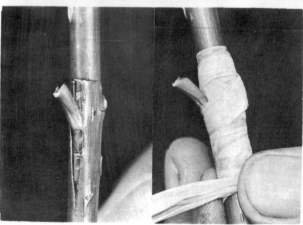

Above—Prepare the bud, retaining a portion of leaf stalk for ease of handling. *Far Left*—Insert the bud into the T-cut, ready for tying. *Near left*—Tie round the bud with raffia after insertion. In the spring, following the budding, cut back the rootstock to about 6 in. above the point of budding.

PROPAGATING GOOSEBERRIES

Right—Select young shoots (made in summer) for cuttings, which are best taken in early October. *Below*—Prepare cuttings 10–12 in. long, discarding the thin ends of the shoots. Cut just above a bud at the top, just below a bud at the bottom.

Below left—Remove lower foliage but leave all buds unless bushes are to be grown on a leg, in which case leave only the top four buds. *Below right*—Insert the cuttings 1 ft apart in a trench 6 in. deep, leaving about a third of the cutting above soil level. Firm planting is essential.

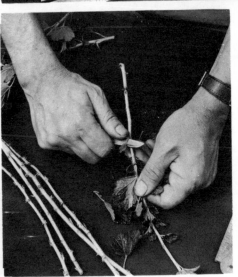

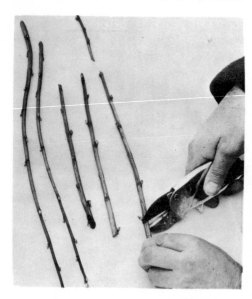

PROPAGATING BLACK
CURRANTS   *Left*—Prepare cutting
8–10 in. long in autumn
using the new shoots made that season. Cu
above a bud at the top, below at the base
Do not use the thin ends of the shoots.

Right—Make a V-slit with a spade alongside
a line. The slit should be 6–7 in. deep.

Left—Insert the cuttings in the slit 1 ft apar
so that only about 2 in. remain above soi
level. Note that all the buds are left intact o
the cuttings.

Right—Make the cuttings firm by treading
alongside and between them.

PROPAGATING STRAWBERRIES

Below—Select a runner which is to be rooted into a pot and cut off the extension to the runner to hasten growth.

Above—Peg down the runner into a 3-in. pot plunged with rim at soil level. When the plant is well rooted, sever it by cutting the runner. Such plants are ideal for re-potting and forcing in the greenhouse.

GRAPES

Below—A single "eye" (bud) can be used for propagation. This is taken from the wood which is pruned from dormant vines in the winter. Stand the pot in a propagating frame in the greenhouse.

BLACKBERRIES

Above—Layering a blackberry shoot in summer. Peg down the end of a young shoot and cover with soil to encourage rooting. Detach layer when rooted and plant separately.

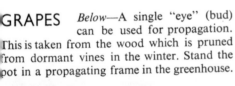

Right—In a cluster of fruit remove the central fruit (king fruit), which is the largest, first. Some fruitlets drop naturally in June, but some further thinning may be required later.

THINNING APPLES AND PEARS

Left—The reason for thinning fruit clusters at an early stage is well shown here. Misshapen and small fruit are the result of not reducing this cluster to two or three fruits only.

Left—Three clusters of pears about to be thinned.

Right—The same clusters after thinning. At a later date these should be further reduced to one fruit per spur.

THINNING APPLES

Left—A typical branch of apple at the correct stage for thinning. Always delay thinning until after the natural shedding of some of the fruitlets in June.

Right — First remove any damaged or misshapen fruit.

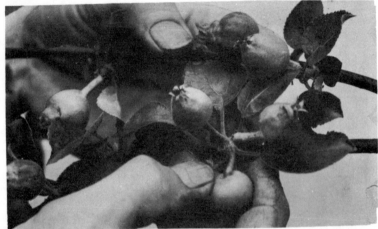

Left—After thinning has been completed. About half the original number of fruits has been removed.

THINNING PEACHES

Left—Typical fruiting branch of peaches on a wall. Note one misshapen flattened fruit against the wire. Thinning should not be done until the stones are formed.   *Below*—After thinning. With an established tree it is usual to leave one fruit per sq. ft of wall space.

THINNING GRAPES AND GOOSEBERRIES

Below left—After thinning it should be possible to push a pencil through a bunch of grapes fairly easily without touching any fruit.   *Below right*—Gooseberries should be thinned when extra large berries are required for exhibition purposes.

MULCHING

Below—Mulching raspberries with compost in early spring. This will help moisture retention —an important point with this crop—and be of manurial value as well.

Above—Black currants and red currants mulched with straw, which is renewed each year so as to be a permanent mulch.

Below—Raspberries mulched with lawn mowings—particularly necessary on a light sandy soil which tends to dry out in summer.

Above—The result of repeatedly cutting off plum suckers just below soil level: the shoot left doubles or trebles itself each time. Cut away suckers from the main root with a knife.

TREATMENT OF DAMAGED BRANCHES

Left—Broken branch caused by a heavy crop of fruit. Such branches should be sawn off cleanly.

Right—After sawing off a branch protect the cut surface with white lead paint or grafting wax.

Left—When a large saw cut is made, pare off the rough edges with a sharp knife before painting the cut surface.

Right—Where branches rub together damage results, and the branch which is least well placed should be removed. Damaged tissue should be painted over.

NEW TREES

Below—When a bundle of fruit trees is received from the nursery, unpack and heel them in (i.e. plant temporarily).

Above—Heel the trees in firmly until they can be set in their final positions.

Below—A vine rod suspended at an angle encourages a more even development of laterals along the length of the rod.

Above—Stopping a vine lateral at the second bud beyond the bunch. One bunch to each lateral is best.

Right—Set a band of paper 6 in. wide in position around the trunk 4 ft from ground level (3 ft for a half-standard).

GREASE BANDS

Left—A grease band traps adult Winter Moths in autumn crawling up the trunks to lay eggs on the branches. Brush off loose bark from the area to which it will be fixed.

Left—Tie the band in place and smear with grease.

Right—Unfruitful trees can sometimes be made to crop by bark ringing. Remove from the main stem two half circles of bark $\frac{1}{2}$ in. wide and cover the cuts with adhesive tape.

CARE OF STRAWBERRIES

Right—Cambridge Favourite planted in September and allowed to fruit the next season, which is usual for cloche- or frame-grown crops. Note the straw, which is put down to keep the fruit clean. *Below*—Strawberries being grown in a barrel. Some plants are set in side holes and some in the open top. Holes are bored in the bottom for drainage.

Above—Remove runners from young plants in summer. This job needs regular attention as fresh shoots appear. *Left*—Young plants out of doors may be de-blossomed in the spring following autumn planting. This gives better crops the following year. Remove the whole flower truss cleanly.

FRUIT IN POTS

Left—Pots for fruit trees should be 14 or 16 in. deep and well crocked to ensure good drainage. Place rough turfy material in the bottom over the crocks.

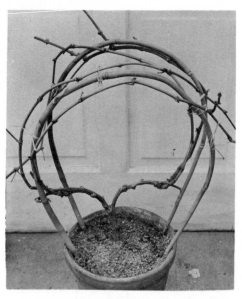

Right—Young grape vine to be trained as an arch in a pot.

Left—Vine rod trained over a strong cane arch. Laterals from the main stem should be pruned back to one bud each winter.

Right—Strawberries in 5-in. pots being forced under glass for an early crop. Young plants used for this purpose should be potted in autumn.

PROTECTION AGAINST BIRDS

Below—Where birds are troublesome protect the fruit buds on an apple tree by covering with small-mesh string netting.

Above—To protect fruiting strawberries against birds hang a net over tightly stretched wires.

Below—Temporary protection can be given to soft fruit by netting suspended on poles, using a jar to prevent the mesh from slipping down the pole.

Above—Fruit tree protected against bird damage to buds by nylon netting.

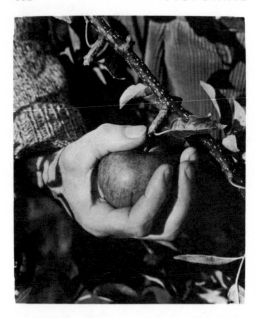

PICKING—I

Left—When the fruit parts readily from the stalk it can be picked. Grasp from below but do not squeeze or bruise.

Right—Exert gentle pressure to detach the fruit. Avoid tearing the stalk roughly from the fruit spur.

Left—When picking avoid damage to the fruit by fingernails. If the fruit does not part easily from the stalk, leave it for a few days.

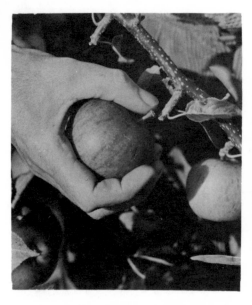

Right—Handle pears with care and pick into a lined basket to avoid bruising.

PICKING—2   *Below*—A picking bag
is useful where a fair
quantity of fruit has to be picked. Use a lined
basket for small quantities.

Above—Pears damaged by brown rot should
be separated from sound fruits. Do not store
damaged fruits.

Below—A good method of apple storage is to
use fibre trays which can be stacked one on the
other. Only sound fruits should be stored.

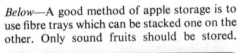

Above—A stripper may be used for picking
black currants in quantity.

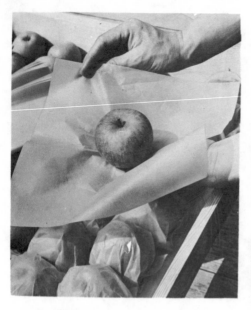

Right—Wrap each fruit this way.

STORING APPLES

Left—Late-keeping dessert varieties can be wrapped in special waxed wraps which prolong storage life. Only perfect fruits should be stored in this way.

Left—Store wrapped fruits in a tray or box. One advantage of wrapping is that rotting fruits are isolated and do not contaminate nearby fruits so readily.

Right—Storage life can be lengthened further by lining and wrapping over the box with polythene.

OTTLING

Right—Most soft fruits, and also plums, green-ages, peaches and pears, can be bottled. Pack e cleaned or peeled fruit evenly into glass reserving jars. A long-handled wooden spoon a useful aid. *Below*—Top up the jars with hot sugar-and-water mixture.

Right—Seal up the jars with spring clips or crew tops. *Below*—Stand 10 min. in a deep an completely immersed in water heated to 80°F, or in an oven at 200°F till the fruit is ender.

Right—Stand the jars for at least 12 hours in he open before testing the seal.

PESTS AND DISEASES—I

Left—Spraying apple trees in winter with ta[r] oil to kill aphids' eggs.

Right—A healthy black currant bush has five veins in the lobe of the leaf.

Left—A bush affected with the virus disease *reversion* has only three veins in the lobe of the leaf.

Right—*Big bud* can cause the spread of reversion. Swollen buds indicate the presence of the pest inside. Pick off these buds and burn them. Also spray with lime sulphur in spring when the leaves are the size of a florin.

PESTS AND DISEASES—2

Below—Apple blossom weevil larvae feed inside the blossom bud. Petals turn brown and do not open. Apply BHC at bud burst stage.

Below—Sawfly larvae cause damage similar to that of codlin moth. Control measure: spray with BHC when 80 per cent of the petals have fallen.

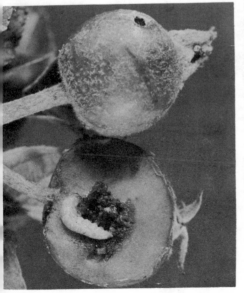

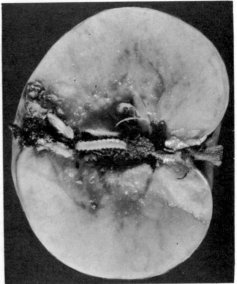

Above—Codlin moth larvae feeding inside a fruit in summer. One of the best control measures in the garden is to spray the trees with derris in mid and late June.

Above—Apple scab can be serious in a wet season. Spray with a captan preparation in spring when damage is anticipated and continue fortnightly throughout the growing season.

Left—A severe attack of apple mildew in dry weather checks the growth of young shoots. Spray with Karathane at first sign of attack.

Below—Brown rot is worst in a wet season. The shrivelled fruits must be gathered and burned to prevent re-infection the following season.

Above—Cane spot disease on a blackberry leaf. Spray with a copper fungicide in mid-May and mid-June.

Right—Canker on an apple shoot. This disease is worst in heavy or wet soils. Pare away damaged tissue and paint over the area with a proprietary preservative material.

PESTS AND DISEASES—4

Below—To cure magnesium deficiency in apples spray foliage with 1 oz. magnesium sulphate in 3 gal. of water at petal fall stage.

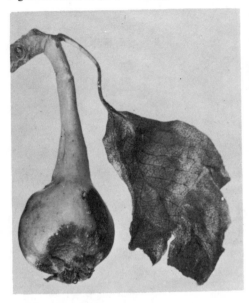

Above—Pear midge larvae can severely damage fruitlets. One of the best control measures is to spray the trees with BHC in the white bud stage.

Below—Control scale insects by spraying the trees with tar oil when dormant in winter.

Above—Magpie moth caterpillars on gooseberries. Control with derris dusts or sprays at first sign of attack. Use the same measures against gooseberry sawfly caterpillars.

PESTS AND DISEASES—5

Left—Aphids on an apple shoot. All species cause damage by sucking sap. Control measures: spray with derris or BHC in summer or a tar oil wash in winter to kill the eggs.

Below—Woolly aphis. Spray with nicotine or BHC at good pressure. Small colonies can be killed by painting with methylated spirit.

Above—Leaves severely damaged by aphids. Spray at the first sign of attack, before the leaves become curled or twisted.

Right—Damage to young shoots caused by woolly aphis. Badly affected shoots should be cut off, as buds will probably be damaged.

INDEX

cos, 283
cultivation of, 220
frames, under, 313, 316, 317, 320
greenhouse, 220
planting-out, 283
seedlings, thinning, 258
Lilac, dead heads, removal of, 116
Lilies, planting, 100
Lily of the valley, cultivation of, 233
Lime, application of, 254
testing for, 254
Lithops, cultivation of, 239
Living stones, cultivation of, 239
Lobelia, planting, 74
sowing, 224
Loganberries, cutting back, 327
planting, 327
Lupins, cuttings of, 175
sowing, 164

M

Machine, aerating lawns by, 34
cutting lawns by, 32, 33
setting of a grass cutting, 35
sowing grass by, 22
Magnesium deficiency in apples, 359
Malus, pruning, 115
Marrows, cloches, under, 309
frames, under, 316
pollination of, 284
slugs, protection from, 284
soil for, 284
Melons, under cloches, 309
frames, 316
Mesembryanthemum, planting, 73
Michaelmas daisies, division of, 191
thinning shoots of, 59
Mimosa pudica, raising from seed, 239
Mint, planting, 260
Moss, use with bulbs, 247
Mulches, for black currants, 345
dahlias, 78
fruit trees, 322
herbaceous borders, 58
materials for, 58
raspberries, 345
red currants, 345
Muscari, planting, 100
Mushrooms, compost for, 285
frames, under, 320
picking, 285
spawn of, 285
Mustard and cress, forcing, 265
Myosotis, *see* Forget-me-nots

N

Narcissus, after-flowering treatment of, 96
bowls of, 244, 248
planting, 95

storing, 96
Nasturtiums, pots of, 109
Nemesia, planting, 73
Nicotiana, planting, 73

O

Onions, bolting, 286
cloches, under, 306, 308
feeding, 267
frames, under, 320
pests of, 274
sets, planting, 286
spring, 286
staging, 295
storing, 298, 301
Welsh, planting, 260
Onion hoe, use of, 258

P

Paeonies, division of, 190
Pansies, planting, 65
Papaver, root cuttings of, 185
Parsnips, planting, 290
thinning, 290
Paths, crazy paving, 15
making, 13, 14
types of, 15
Peaches, bottling, 355
fan trained, 334
thinning fruits of, 344
training, 334
Pears, bottling, 355
budding, 338
picking, 352, 353
thinning fruit of, 343
Peas, birds, protection against, 276
cloches, under, 305
mulches for, 287
staging, 295
staking, 287
weevil, protection from, 274
Pelargonium, *see* Geranium
Peperomia, leaf cuttings of, 183
Perennials, sowing, 162, 164
Pergolas, construction of, 16–18
Pests:
aphids, apple, 356, 360
black bean, 273
big bud, black currant, 356
blossom weevil, apple, 357
cabbage white butterfly, 273
carrot fly, 274
caterpillar damage, 143
codling moth, apple, 357
eelworm, phlox, 188
flea beetle, brassica, 275
fumigation against, 217
gall weevil, cabbage, 273